Windows 10 – Improving Privacy & Security

TYLER S. PAYNE

ABOUT THE AUTHOR

Tyler Payne has worked in the IT field for over a decade. During this time, he has worked for a Fortune 500 company and has provided expert level consulting to multiple Fortune 100 companies. Including, services in Cyber and Technology to the Air Force, Army, and Navy.

As a contractor for the Air Force, he took part in verifying vulnerabilities within an F-15 Fighter Jet System at the Pentagon in Washington D.C. His current area of expertise is information protection, system survivability, and hardening, for the United States Air Force.

He has studied Associates of Arts in General Studies and Bachelors of Science in Cybersecurity at American Military University. Tyler's certifications consist of: CompTIA A+, CompTIA Security+, Microsoft Certified Technology Specialist (MCTS), CompTIA Advanced Security Practitioner (CASP), and (ISC)² Certified Information Systems Security Professional (CISSP).

DEDICATION

I would like to dedicate this book to my wife. Tiffany, you have always been there for me day in and day out. Whether it has been taking care of our children while I was working on this book, taking care of our home while working towards my degree, holding down the fort while I studied for certifications, you have been the core to our home, family, and relationship. I know you don't hear this enough, thank you for always doing the best you can with every obstacle in our path. I love you!

www.TylerPayne.com

Table of Contents

Scenario: Imagine you have been working hard on a major project for work/school or maybe you have an enormous number of pictures, videos, and personal documents (taxes, passwords, etc.) stored on your computer. How would you feel if one day you discovered the computer which contained all of this information has been hacked or stolen? If this was my computer, I would feel sick to my stomach knowing someone now has free and open access to all of my personal information. However, if you would have taken just 30 minutes to properly configure the settings of your Windows 10 system, you could have significantly mitigated the loss of your personal information and privacy.

Everything in life is a risk decision, and just about every risk can be mitigated by knowledge and action. When you get in a car you are at risk. However, you mitigate this risk by wearing a seat belt. When you have delicate and personal information stored on a computer, you are at risk. However, you can mitigate this risk by applying the methods you will learn throughout this book.

CHAPTER 01 – BIOS Mode

In this chapter, you will learn what Basic Input Output Software (BIOS) Mode a system is utilizing and how you can use it to improve and enhance the security configuration of a computer.

BIOS Mode Overview

Computers use two different types of BIOS configurations. The configurations are either BIOS Legacy or Unified Extensible Firmware Interface (UEFI). Depending on what type of BIOS the computer is using will define the "BIOS Mode" for which Windows 10 will operate with. In most cases, the modern computer will be using UEFI as the BIOS Mode. Older computers most likely will be using the older version of BIOS called BIOS Legacy. The BIOS simply is responsible for setting up the computer at the lowest level. It will go through four phases during setup which are Power-On-Self-Test (POST), Setup, Bootstrap Loader, and Drivers.

During the POST phase, the computer will test the internal hardware. This test ensures there are no issues with the hardware such as the memory. If there is an issue, the computer will beep or provide an error code that will point a technician to the correct maintenance action.

After the POST phase is complete the computer will begin to initialize the remaining actions as directed by the configuration within the BIOS setup. There are a few configurations that we will get into throughout this book. Such as disabling the CMOS Camera (Laptop Built-in Camera). The setup will dictate whether or not the internal camera should be on or off. You can also disable the computers Universal Serial Bus (USB) ports within the BIOS setup menu.

During the BIOS setup, the computer will also perform the Bootstrap Loader phase. This is when the computer will determine if there is an operating system. Once an operating system is found the computer will pass control to it after the initialization process is complete.

While the computer is dealing with **BIOS** setup and Bootstrap Loader, the computer hardware drivers are being loaded. Drivers allow the operating system to interact with hardware.

Navigate to BIOS Mode

Step 1: Click on the "Search Icon" or inside the "Search Box" on the lower taskbar.

Step 2: Type "System Information" and hit enter.

Step 3: In the right pane under "Item", look for "BIOS Mode".

Note: It will either say "Legacy" which is the older **BIOS** or it will say "UEFI" which is the most current **BIOS** Mode.

How to Access UEFI (BIOS Mode)

Method #1

Step 1: Turn on the computer and press either the Escape, Delete, F2, F10, or F12 key.

Step 2: Enter the Setup/BIOS/UEFI.

Note: You only need to select one key. This key is dependent upon the manufacture make/model of the computer. You can perform a quick Internet search for your specific computer or try each key until you find it.

Method #2

Step 1: Click the Windows (Start) icon in the lower left-hand corner of the computer screen.

Step 2: Click on the Settings icon.

Step 3: In the "Windows Settings" window, click on Update & Security.

Step 4: Under Update & Security, click on Recovery.

Step 5: Click Restart Now under Advanced Startup. The computer will now restart.

Step 6: Click Troubleshoot under Choose an Option.

Step 7: Click Advanced Options under Troubleshoot

Step 8: Click UEFI Firmware Settings in the Advanced Options window.

Step 9: Click Restart in the UEFI Firmware Settings window.

Start > Settings > Update & Security > Recovery > Restart Now > Troubleshoot > Advanced Options > UEFI Firmware Settings > Restart

UEFI (BIOS) Settings

Setting UEFI Password

We are going to set what is called the Administrator and User Password. These two passwords are strictly used for the UEFI interface. These passwords protect the UEFI and computer from malicious activity. When the computer turns on you will immediately be presented with an interface requesting you to "Enter Password". At this point, you can either enter the Administrator or User password.

The Administrator password allows you to access the UEFI to initialize, access the interface, make changes to the setup, and load the Windows 10 OS. The User password only allows the UEFI to initialize and then loads the Windows 10 OS.

Therefore, by setting the Administrator and User password you can significantly reduce the likelihood of someone being able to access the Windows 10 OS as well as the UEFI settings.

Step 1: Follow one of the steps above to enter the UEFI.

Step 2: Navigate to the advance settings page (F7)

Step 3: Click on the Security tab.

Step 3: Under the Security tab you will see the Administrator and User Password. Go ahead and set two separate passwords for the Administrator and User accounts.

Step 4: You should now see the Administrator and User password status showing as "Installed".

Step 5: Proceed over to Save & Exit to save and exit. You might have to hit F-10 on the keyboard to Save & Exit.

Step 5: The computer should now restart prompting you for a password immediately as shown in Figure 1.2. You can also go back into the UEFI and test the Administrator or Supervisor password as well.

Note: If you want to make UEFI setting modifications you will need to enter the Administrator Password on this screen. If you wish to just move forward with booting to the Windows 10 OS, then you should enter the User Password.

Boot Order

The "Boot Order" is the 1, 2, and 3 for how the computer is instructed to boot. You can instruct the computer to first boot from a CD, then USB, and finally Hard Drive. The computer will turn on and check to see if there is a CD in the computer. If so, the computer will boot from it. If there is no CD, the computer will proceed to boot option #2 and check to see if there is a USB to boot from. If there is no USB the computer will then proceed to boot option #3 and check to see if there is a Hard Drive to boot from. For this effort, we are looking at security. Therefore, we will only utilize one boot option, which shall be the Hard Drive.

Why do we want to remove the other options? There are "Live" CDs (Kali Linux) which are used to unlock accounts, crack passwords, and promote privileges for user accounts. Once an attacker has physical access to your computer, they can simply insert one of these live CDs or USBs into the computer. Instead of booting to Windows 10, they will boot to this "Live CD". From here they can create new user accounts or remove your password from the account. At this point, they can either log into the computer as you or with the new account they have created. After logging in, they can then access all of your personal information stored on the computer. This is why it's important to ensure we have set the computer to boot only from the internal hard drive.

Step 1: Boot the system into the UEFI settings.

Step 2: Navigate to the Advanced (F7) portion of the UEFI.

Step 3: Click on the Boot Options tab.

Step 4: You will see "Boot Option #1". Set this to your internal Hard Drive.

Step 5: If you have "Boot Option #2" or more, you will need to click each one and set it to "Disabled".

Step 6: Navigate to Save and Exit or press F10 on your keyboard.

Step 7: Go back into the UEFI setting and verify the changes are set.

Secure Boot

Secure Boot is a great security feature protecting the system integrity and providing the user assurance their system is "Securely Booting". There are many different types of malware floating around the world today. The biggest threat to the system is a type of malware that loads before the Windows 10 OS. These types of malware are referred to as Boot-Kits and Root-Kits. This type of malware loads before the operating system. They are undetectable by traditional malware scanning software.

If the computer that has UEFI and a Trusted Platform Module (TPM) can use the "Secure Boot" feature. This ensures the computer loads only a trusted operating system and for our effort, we want to ensure the Windows 10 OS is booting securely within the system.

CMOS Camera

The "CMOS Camera" is the computer built-in camera (if it has one). If you do not utilize the camera on your computer, you will want to disable it. However, we go a bit further and disable the camera at a much lower level than the Windows 10 OS. This provides a pretty good assurance that if a hacker were to compromise your system, they would be unable to spy on you as they would need lower system-level permissions to activate the camera. In most situations, they would need physical access to the computer to turn the camera back on.

Step 1: Boot the system into the UEFI.

Step 2: Navigate to the Advanced (F7) portion of the UEFI.

Step 3: Navigate to the Advanced Tab.

Step 4: Click on Security.

Step 5: Click on I/O Interface Security.

Step 6: Click on USB Interface Security.

Step 7: Click on CMOS Camera and change the setting to Lock.

<u>**Step 8:**</u> Save changes and exit (F10).

<u>**Step 9:**</u> Go back into the UEFI and validate the settings we have just made.

BIOS Mode Review

As you can see, the UEFI has many settings that can help protect your data from theft, such as setting the UEFI passwords. You can also prevent hackers from spying on you by disabling the CMOS Camera. And then there is the Secure Boot feature which prevents malware from installing itself at a much lower process than the operating system.

CHAPTER 02 – User Accounts

In this chapter, you will learn what User Accounts are on the Windows 10 OS and how you should use them to mitigate your risk to special attacks and vulnerabilities.

User Accounts Overview

Whenever you log into a computer, you are operating with certain permissions that are assigned to the user account. There are two types of user accounts we will be discussing for Windows 10. They are referred to as the "Standard User Account" and "Privileged User Account". The privileged user account is most commonly known as the Administrator or Admin account. This type of account can install software and make system-level changes. The "Standard User Account" is not a privileged user account. The standard account can launch items such as Microsoft Word, Internet Explorer, and Calculator. However, this account cannot install or uninstall software. It cannot make system-level changes.

Standard User Account

Standard user accounts are generally more restricted than a privileged user account. Meaning, you should have less permission and capability than the privileged user account. You should not be able to install software or change major system settings on a computer while operating under the standard user account. This is very important! Many viruses and malware require special permission to install itself onto the computer. This typically requires a privileged user account (administrator) to carry out the task. However, by using the standard user account (least privileged), you can prevent this type of malicious software from carrying out an attack. Ultimately, by using the standard user account you lower your risk of exposing the computer to infection/compromise.

Privileged User Account

The privileged user account has more privileges than the standard user account. This account typically has the permissions to install software, uninstall software, and modify system settings. This can be a very dangerous account if used improperly by unexperienced individuals. The golden rule of using a privileged user account is to only use this account when needing to make changes to the system's settings. If you are not performing "administrator" activities, then you should be using a standard user account.

The goal is to lower your risk of infection/compromise. If you are logged into the computer as a privileged user and accidentally download a malicious file you could easily compromise the computer because the file will have exactly what it needs to execute itself. After all, you are the admin. The Department of Defense requires all "Administrators" to maintain two accounts. These administrators have their privileged user account for performing "Administrator" duties as well as their standard user account for creating documents in word, responding to emails, and browsing the internet.

Navigate to User Accounts

What User Account Do I Have?

The first thing you should understand is what account privileges you are operating with. Follow the steps below to determine what local accounts you have on the system.

<u>**Step 1:**</u> Click on the Windows "Start" Icon.

<u>**Step 2:**</u> Scroll down to the "Windows System" folder and click the arrow to expand.

<u>**Step 3:**</u> Click on "Control Panel".

Step 4: Click on "User Accounts".

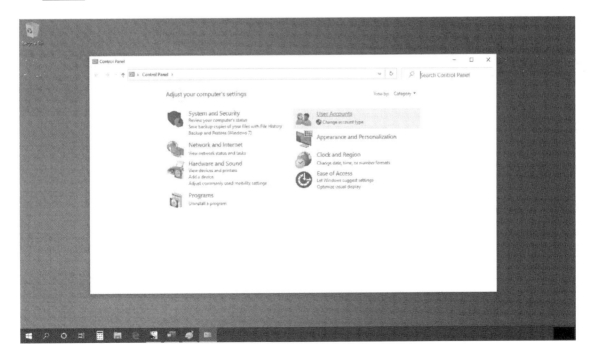

Step 5: Click on "Change Account Type".

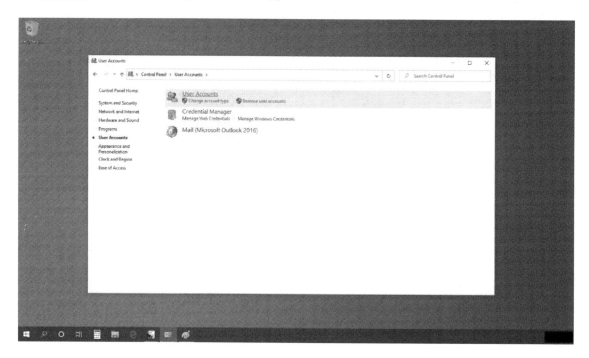

Step 6: Click on the current logged in account. For this example, we will click on "Tyler Standard".

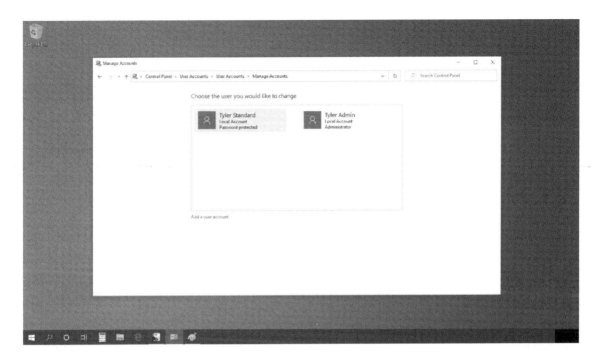

Step 7: Click on "Change the account type".

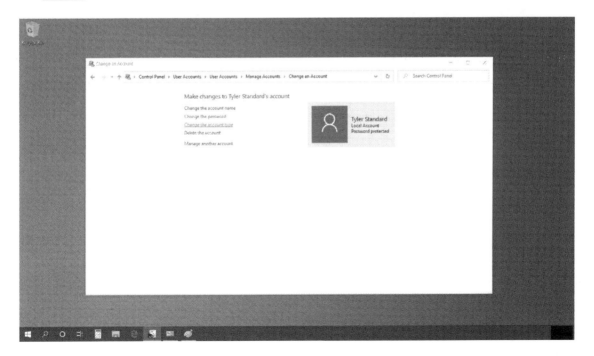

Step 8: From here you can see if the "Standard" or "Administrator" account is selected. In this example, the "Standard" account is selected.

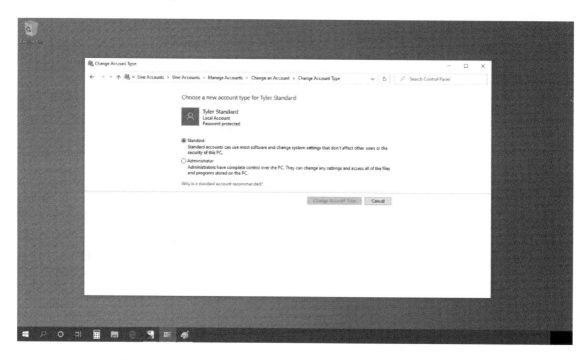

Note: Here you can see I have named my login account as "Tyler Standard". This helps me visually see what account I am selecting before I log into the computer. However, if you have never created a new account since purchasing your computer, you are most likely operating with the Administrator account.

User Account Settings

Creating a Standard User Account

Step 1: Click on the Windows "Start" Icon.

Step 2: Scroll down to the "Windows System" folder and click the arrow to expand.

Step 3: Click on "Control Panel".

Step 4: Click on "User Accounts".

Step 5: Click on "User Accounts" again.

Step 6: Click on "Manage Another Account".

Step 7: Click on "Add a user account".

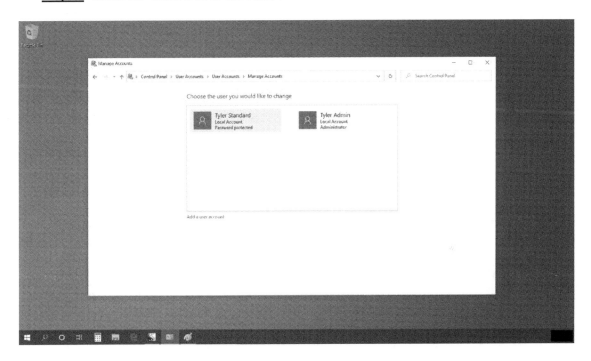

Step 8: At the bottom, click on "Sign in without a Microsoft Account (not recommended)".

Note: This selection says "not recommended". However, Microsoft would like for you to use their Microsoft Cloud account feature, where they store your credentials online. However, I am not a fan of my credentials being stored online. Therefore, I recommend creating a local account, which is stored locally in the system.

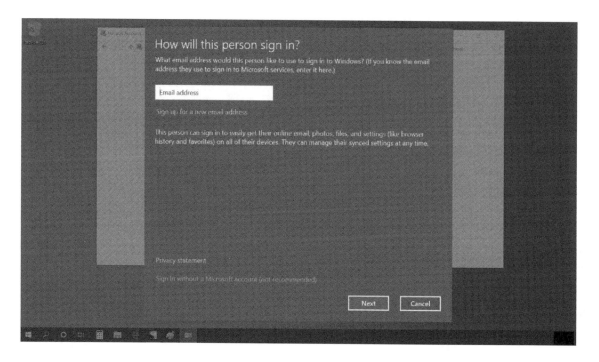

Step 9: At the bottom, click on "Local account".

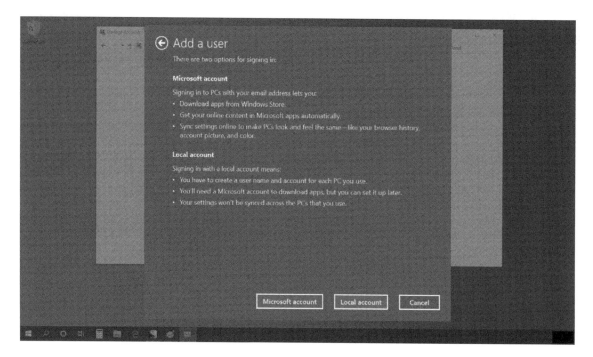

Step 10: Fill in the "User name, Password, and Password hint. Click Next when complete".

Step 11: Click on "Finish".

Step 12: You should now be back at the "Manage Accounts" window. You should now have the new user account on the system.

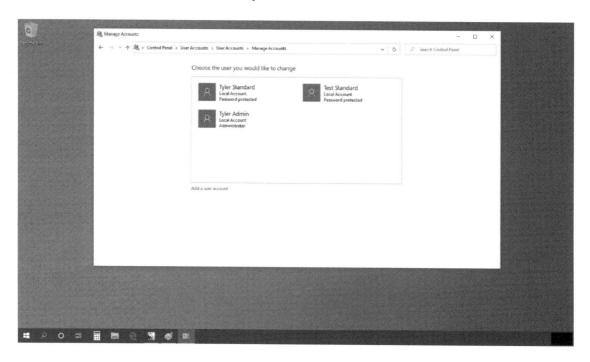

Creating a Privileged User Account

Step 1: Click on the Windows "Start" Icon.

Step 2: Scroll down to the "Windows System" folder and click the arrow to expand.

Step 3: Click on "Control Panel".

Step 4: Click on "User Accounts".

Step 5: Click on "User Accounts" again.

Step 6: Click on "Manage Another Account".

Step 7: Click on "Add a user account".

Step 8: At the bottom, click on "Sign in without a Microsoft Account (not recommended)".

Note: This selection says "not recommended". However, Microsoft would like for you to use their Microsoft Cloud account feature, where they store your credentials online. However, I am not a fan of my credentials being stored online. Therefore, I recommend creating a local account, which is stored locally in the system.

Step 9: At the bottom, click on "Local account".

Step 10: Fill in the "User name, Password, and Password hint. Click Next when complete".

Step 11: Click on "Finish".

Step 12: You should now be back at the "Manage Accounts" window. You should now have the new user account on the system.

Step 13: With the "Manage Account" window still open, click on the new account you just created. For this example, I will click on "Test Admin".

Step 14: Click on "Change the Account Type".

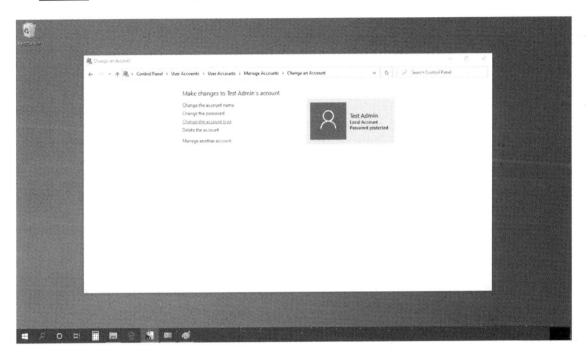

Step 15: As you can see the account defaulted to the "Standard" account.

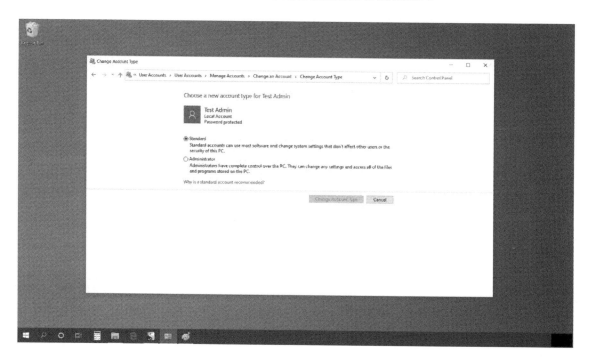

Step 16: Click the "Administrator" circle box and click the "Change Account Type".

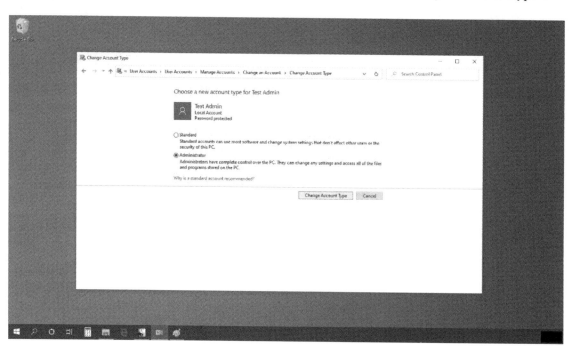

Step 17: You should now see the account name showing "Local account - Administrator".

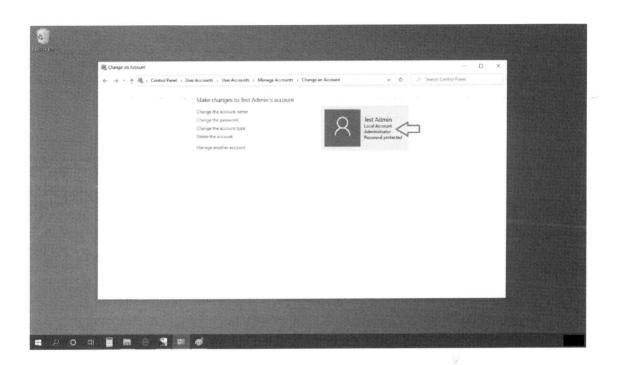

User Accounts Review

In this chapter, we discussed user accounts and explained the difference between a local standard user account and a local privileged user account. It is recommended to only use the privileged user account when needing to install software or making system changes. For browsing the internet, sending emails, and creating word documents, it is recommended to only use the standard user account. Using a standard user account helps mitigate your risk (exposure) to malicious software such as malware/viruses.

CHAPTER 03 – BitLocker

In this chapter, you will learn about BitLocker and how to effectively use BitLocker to protect personal information from theft.

BitLocker Overview

BitLocker is a program developed by Microsoft used to provide Data at Rest (DAR) protection, using full-disk encryption. This program can protect data from unauthorized access on the computer.

Full Disk Encryption

Full disk encryption is used to secure the entire disk space. If you have a hard drive with 500 GB of space; all space (including unused) will be encrypted. This protects everything on the hard drive. With full-disk encryption, the hard drive is either in an encrypted state or a decrypted state. Once the hard drive is decrypted, all the data becomes available.

BitLocker Requirements

Not every Windows 10 OS has the capability to use BitLocker. We will quickly identify if your computer meets BitLocker requirements.

Step 1: You must be running Windows 10 Pro, Education, or Enterprise Edition to use Microsoft BitLocker. Microsoft Windows 10 Home does not provide BitLocker capability. I recommend you upgrade to the Windows 10 Pro version as BitLocker is a great feature for safeguarding and protecting your personal information.

Step 2: BitLocker requires the computer to have a Trusted Platform Module (TPM) version 1.2 or higher. This is a special chip on the motherboard of the computer.

Check the TPM Version

Here we will identify what TPM version you have.

Step 1: Right-click the start icon.

Step 2: Click on "Device Manager".

Step 3: Click on the "Security Devices" dropdown.

Step 4: It should say "Trusted Platform Module" followed by a number such as 1.2, 2.0, or better.

Installing BitLocker

The following will explain how to install BitLocker on a computer that meets the BitLocker requirements.

Step 1: In the search window type "BitLocker" and press enter.

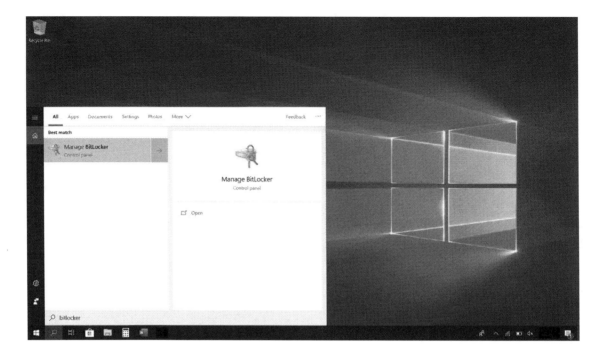

Step 2: Click on "System and Security".

Step 3: Click on "BitLocker Drive Encryption".

Step 4: The BitLocker Drive Encryption window will open. Under Operating System Drive click on "Turn on BitLocker". This is usually going to be next to the C: drive.

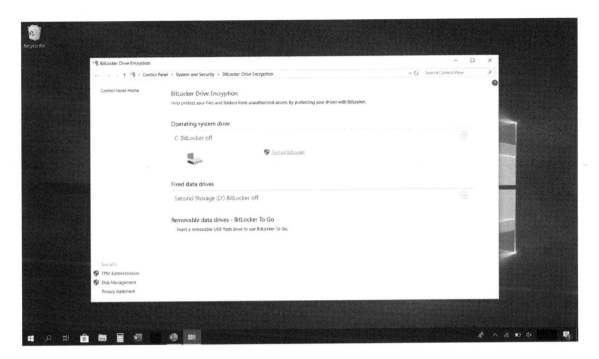

Step 5: You will be asked "How do you want to back up your recovery key?".

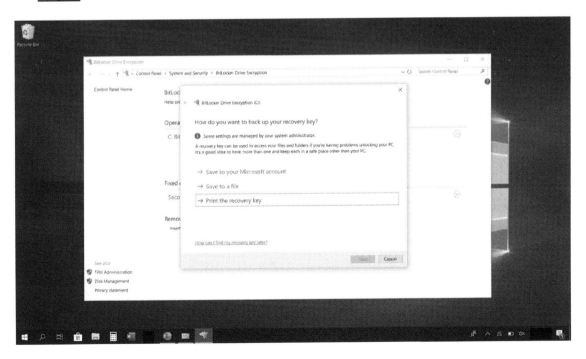

Step 6: You will want to click on "Print the recovery key" and click next.

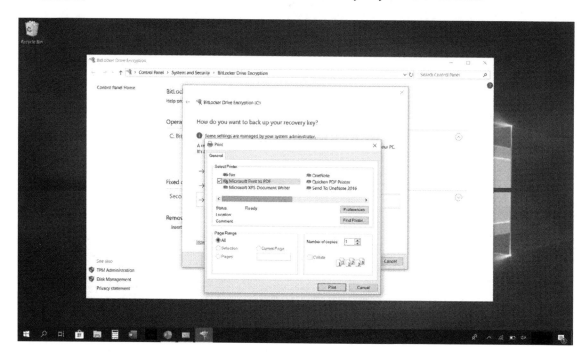

Step 7: If you have a printer then go ahead and print the recovery key and lock it in a safe. If you do not have a printer then you will want to choose print to PDF. This is very important! We will set an easier password later in this guide. However, if you forget the password, this key is your only hope of getting back into the hard drive after it becomes encrypted. From here you will want to save the created PDF file to a USB device. Click next when finished.

Step 8: You should now be at "Choose how much of your drive to encrypt". I would choose "Encrypt entire drive". Click next.

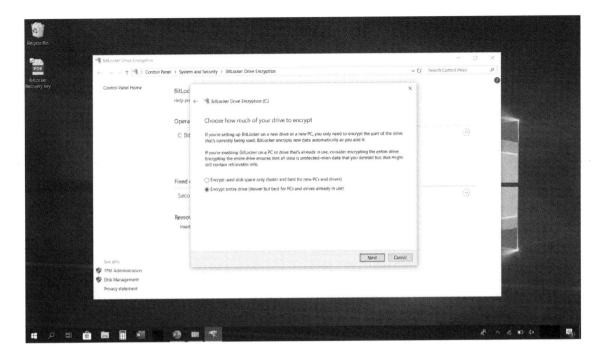

Step 9: From the "Choose which encryption mode to use", click on "New encryption mode" and click next.

Step 10: You will need to make sure the checkbox is checked for the "Run BitLocker system check" and press continue.

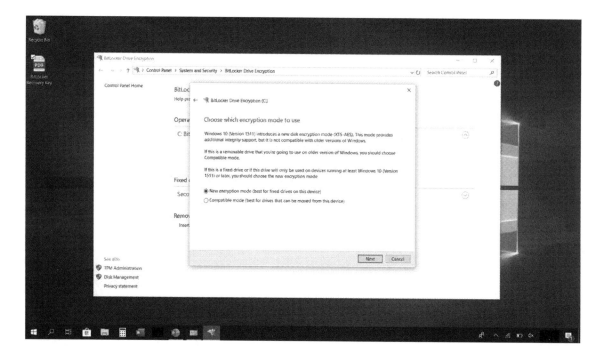

Step 11: From the "Are you ready to encrypt this drive?", you will want to ensure the box is checked for the "Run BitLocker system check". Press Continue when ready.

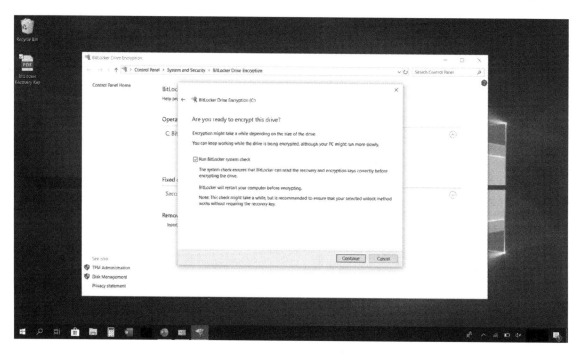

Step 12: A window will open stating "The computer must be restarted". Press "Restart Now".

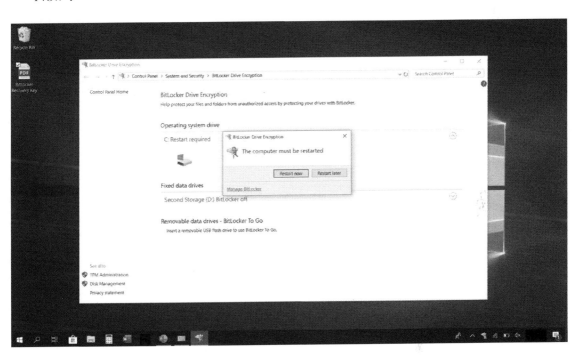

Step 13: After the computer has finished restarting, you will need to go back into Control Panel > System and Security > BitLocker Drive Encryption. Under the "Operating system drive", you will see the C: drive. It should say "BitLocker Encrypting". This means BitLocker is now encrypting the drive. This could take a while depending on how large the drive is.

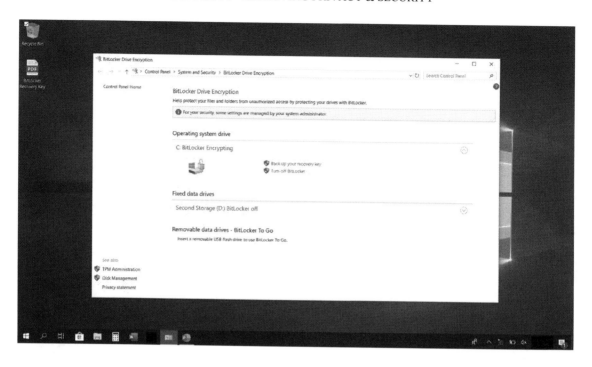

Step 14: Now we are going to see what percent of the drive is encrypted. Click on the search icon and type "CMD", Right-click "Command Prompt" and click "Run as administrator".

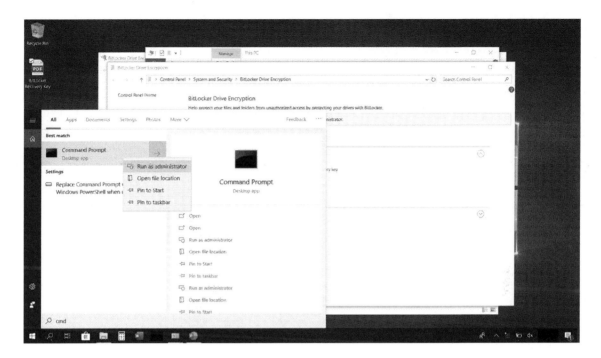

Step 15: Inside the command prompt you will need to type "manage-bde -status" and hit enter. This will show you the hard drive Size, BitLocker Version, Conversion Status, and Percentage Encrypted. If you look for "Volume C: and look at Percentage Encrypted, you will see it is at 24.3% in the picture below. You should be able to see the percentage for your system on your command prompt window as well.

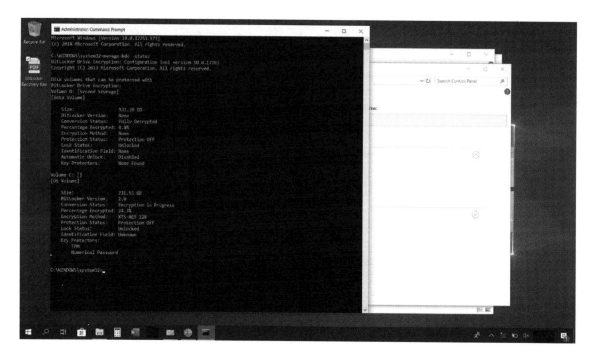

Step 16: Once the percentage is at 100% you will see the "Protection Status" set to "Protection On". This means BitLocker is now protecting the hard drive. Unfortunately, we are not done just yet.

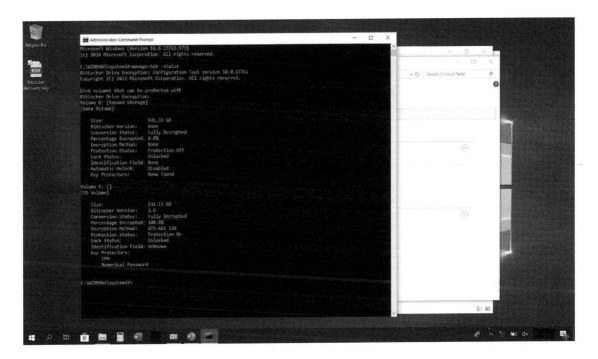

Step 17: Click on search and type "gpedit.msc" click "Run as administrator".

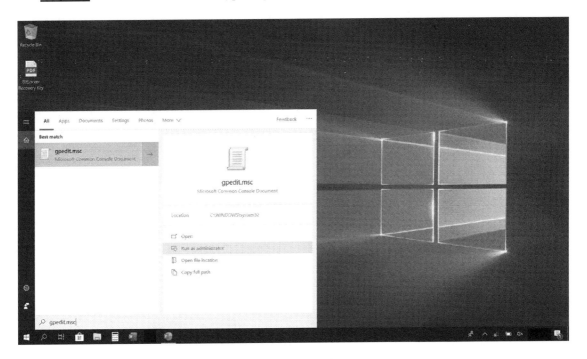

Step 18: The "Local Group Policy Editor" window will open.

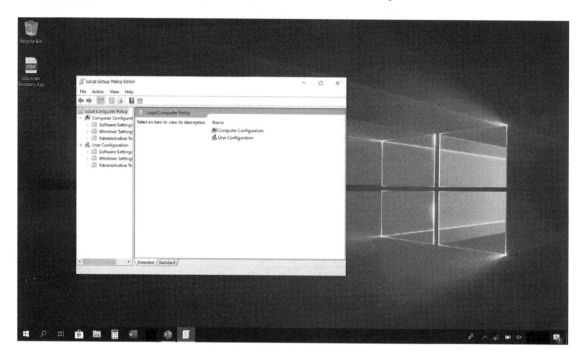

Step 19: Under "Local Computer Policy" navigate to: Computer Configuration > Administrative Templates > Window Components > BitLocker Drive Encryption > Operating System Drives.

Step 20: Click and open "Require additional authentication at startup" on the right pane of the window.

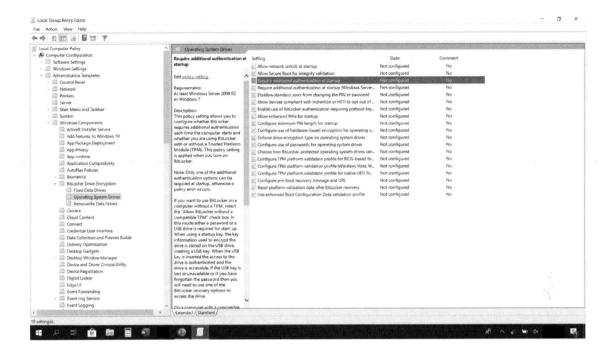

Step 21: In the "Require additional authentication at startup" window, click Enabled. Under the Options: for "Configure TPM startup PIN:" select "Require startup PIN with TPM and click OK. Close the window.

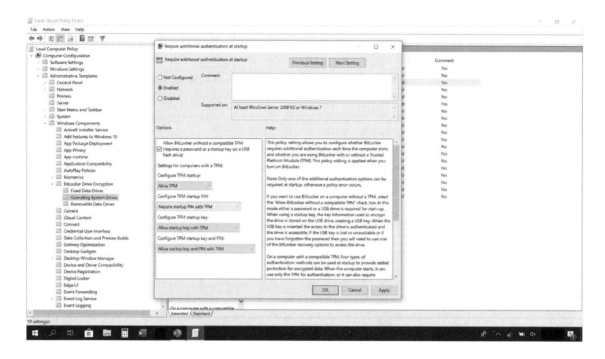

Step 22: Back in the command prompt you will want to type "manage-bde -protectors -add c: -TPMandPIN" and press enter.

Step 23: You will now be asked to "Type the PIN to use to protect the volume:". You will want to type a numerical PIN and press enter. You will be asked to "Confirm the PIN by typing it again:". Type the same PIN and press enter.

Step 24: The window should now show "Key Protectors Added" as well as the TPM and PIN IDs.

Step 25: In the command prompt type "manage-bde -status" and hit enter. Under Volume C: you can find "Key Protectors:". This should now show "Numerical Password, TPM, and PIN".

Step 26: Exit the command prompt window and perform a restart of the system. You should now be presented with a BitLocker window asking for the PIN you just set. Type in the PIN and press enter. The computer should now begin to boot.

Congratulations! You now have BitLocker protecting your data!

BitLocker Review

BitLocker is a great tool developed by Microsoft to protect your data by using encryption. This security enhancement will most certainly protect your data from physical theft.

CHAPTER 04 – Cortana

In this chapter, we will be discussing what "Cortana" is and how it can be used by attackers when not properly configured.

Cortana Overview

Cortana is Microsoft's "Virtual Assistant". Think of Cortana like you would "Alexa" or "Siri". Cortana can find files, search for information on the Internet, play music, manage your calendar, listen for command words, and many other special tasks. Cortana is an advanced search and task organizer.

However, Cortana can also be used by attackers (hackers) to perform quick and efficient data extraction from your computer. It has access to your calendar, it can listen into your device, and perform advance file searches for videos, pictures, and special document extensions such as excel, pdf, word. If Cortana is "always" listening to special command words like "Hey Cortana!", then attackers can utilize this feature and have it trigger from words like "My credit card number is .....", you know that moment when you whip out your credit card and provide the details over the phone.

Navigate to Cortana

Step 1: Click on the "Start" icon in the lower left-hand corner of the taskbar.

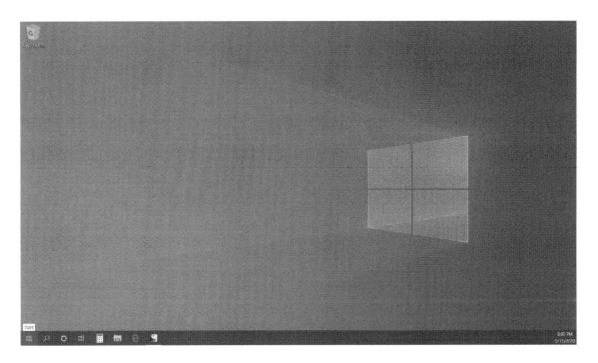

Step 2: Click on "Settings".

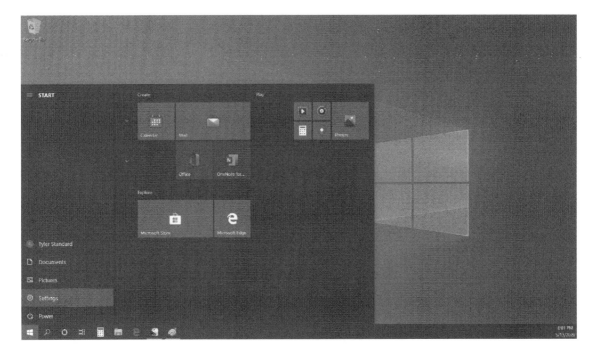

<u>**Step 3:**</u> Click on "Cortana".

Cortana Settings

After you have navigated to Cortana. You will see multiple links on the left of the window such as:

- Talk to Cortana
- Permissions
- More Details

Talk to Cortana

In this Window you will see:

- Hey Cortana
- Keyboard Shortcut

- Lock Screen

Make sure each setting has been set to off.

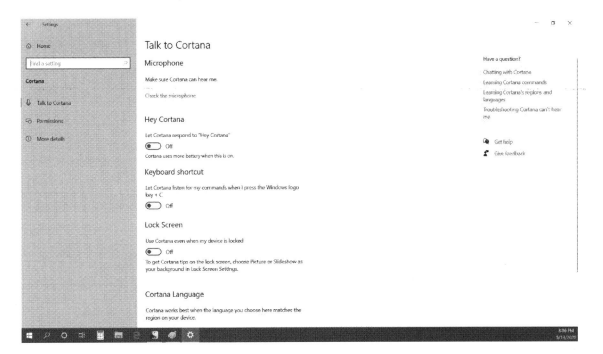

Permissions

Under the Permissions section, you will need to click on "Manage the information Cortana can access from this device". You will then see:

- Location
- Contacts, Email, Calendar, & Communication History
- Browsing History

Make sure each setting is set to off.

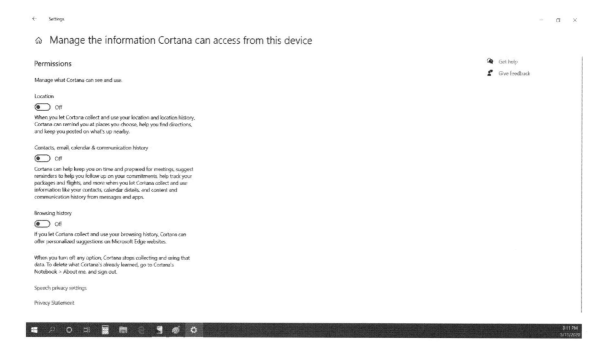

At the bottom of this window you will see "Speech Privacy Settings" you will want to click on this. Make sure "Online Speech Recognition" is set to off. As can see this allows Cortana to use your voice data to improve its speech services. Meaning, your microphone is listening to everything you say.

Cortana Review

Cortana performs as a great "Virtual Assistant". However, you give up a bit of personal privacy when authorizing Cortana to perform as a virtual assistant. I do not like Cortana using my computer's built-in microphone listening for "Special" command words waiting to jump into action. I also do not need Cortana tracking my device history across platforms.

CHAPTER 05– Privacy

In this chapter, we will go over the Privacy settings for Windows 10.

Privacy Overview

Privacy is located under Start > Settings > Privacy. Here we can modify how Microsoft uses our information for Windows 10 and Apps. Settings which can be modified are found under:

- General
- Activity History
- Location
- Camera
- Microphone
- Voice Activation
- Notifications
- Account Info
- Contacts
- Calendar
- Call History
- Email
- Tasks
- Messaging
- Radios
- Other Devices
- Background Apps
- App diagnostics
- Automatic file downloads
- Documents
- Pictures
- Videos
- File System

As you can see, Windows 10 has a list of items we will need to modify to ensure our security and privacy.

Navigate to Privacy

Step 1: Click on "Start".

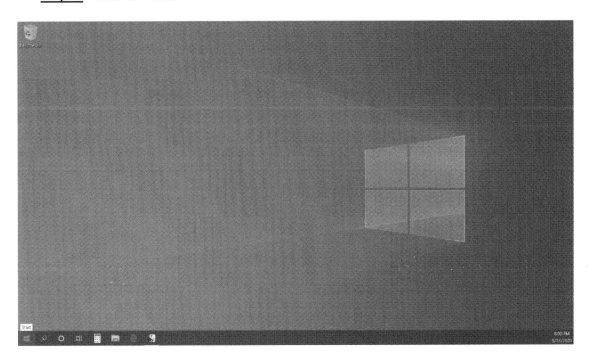

Step 2: Click on "Settings".

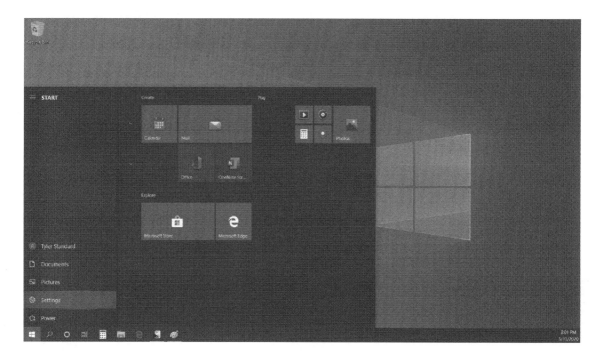

Step 3: Click on "Privacy".

Privacy Settings

General

Under the "General" setting, you will see "Change privacy options". You will want to turn all 4 options off as we do not want to let apps make advertising more interesting, let websites provide locally relevant content, let windows track app launches or all windows to show me suggested content.

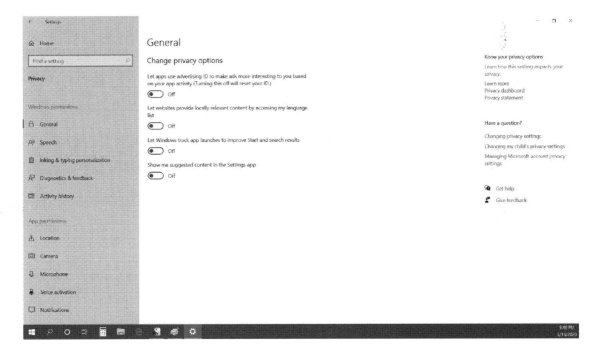

Activity History

Click on "Activity History". From here you will see two checkboxes, which are; "Store my activity history on this device", "Send my activity history to Microsoft". Below that, you will see "Show activities from these accounts". You will want to make sure the two boxes are unchecked and click the "Clear" button of "activity history"; and click okay, to clear the activity history.

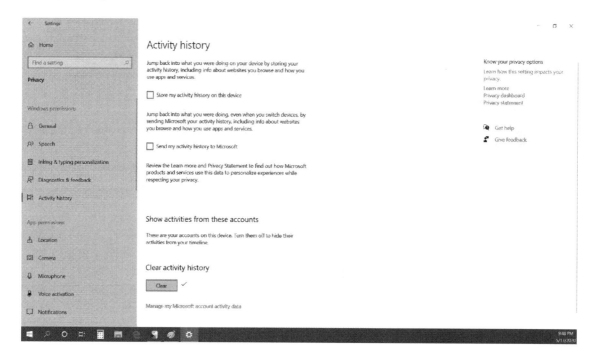

Location

Click on "Location", you will see, "Allow access to location on this device". Click Change and make sure this is set to off. You will also see "Allow apps to access your location". You will want to set this to off. Under "Location History", you will want to click on "Clear". This will clear away any saved information on tracked locations. Under "Choose which apps can access your precise location", make sure each app is set to off.

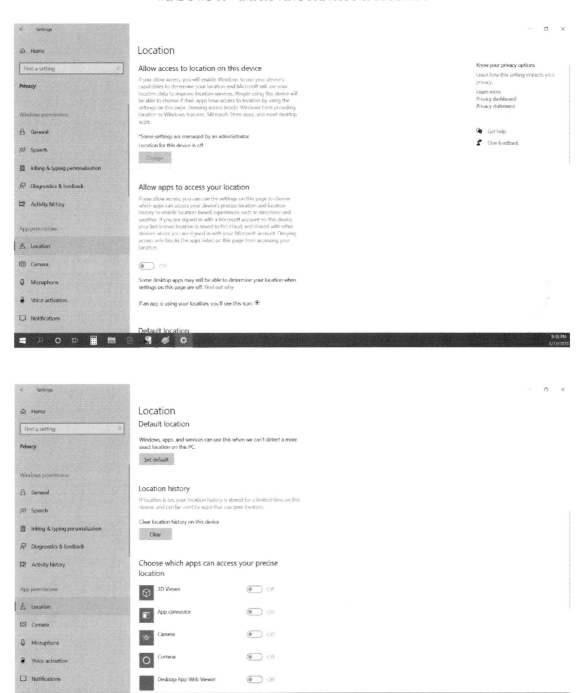

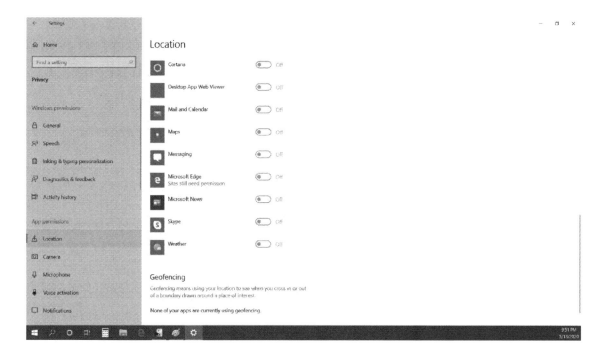

Note: There are many reasons to stop the system from tracking your location. You could take a picture with your Windows 10 device and it will record your location within the metadata of the picture. If you upload this picture the location goes with it. Anyone can see exactly where you took this picture. This also goes for messaging and Skype. People can see where you are if your location is being recorded. If you are on vacation, criminals can you this data to then rob your home. You may think that a nice vacation picture was perfect to share with friends on social media but criminals will use this information against you.

Camera

Click on "Camera", you will see "Allow access to the camera on this device". Earlier we disabled the internal Camera through the UEFI settings. We can also disable the service within the Windows 10 OS. This is called "Defense in Depth". Adding multiple layers of security is known as best practice. So, we will also be disabling the Camera's service. Under "Allow access to the camera on this device" you will want to click the "Change" button and set this to off. Make sure the "Allow apps to access your camera" is also set to off. Under "Choose which Microsoft Store apps can access your camera", set each on to off. Under "Allow desktop apps to access your camera", set this to off.

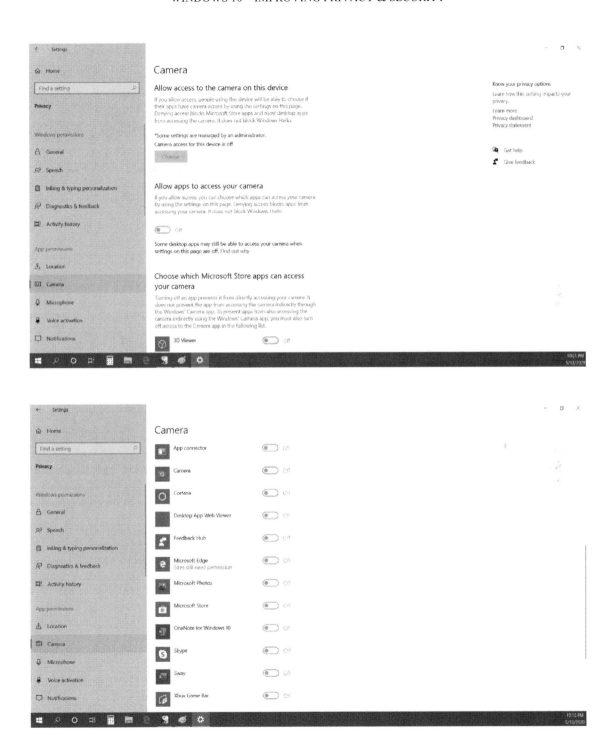

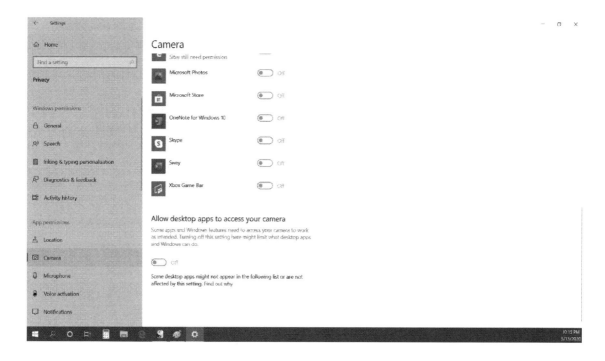

Note: If you use your Camera to communicate with people using apps such as Skype, then you will need to leave the "Allow access to the camera on this device" to on as well as the "Allow apps to access your camera". Under the "Choose which Microsoft Store apps can access your camera", you will need to set the Skype app to "on". However, I do not use my camera to communicate with anyone on my computer. Therefore, I set these settings to off. If you do use this feature, I highly encourage you to come back to this setting and ensure only the right apps have access to your camera.

Microphone

Click on "Microphone", you will see "Allow access to the microphone on this device". You will want to click the "Change" button and set this to off. Under "Allow apps to access your microphone", you will want to set this to off. Under "Choose which Microsoft Store apps can access your microphone", you will want to set each app to off. Under "Allow desktop apps to access your microphone", you will want to set this setting to off.

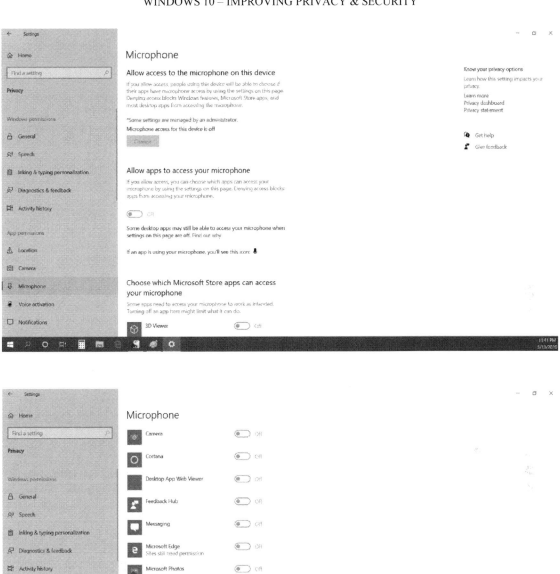

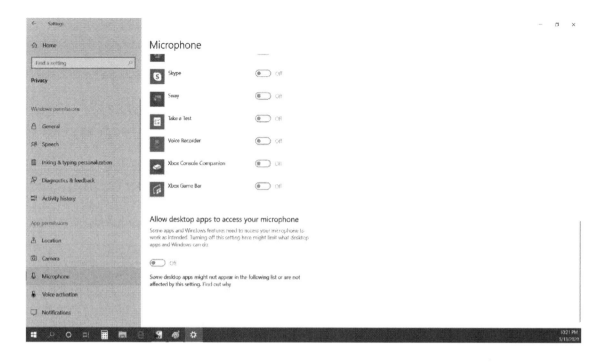

Note: If you use your Microphone to communicate with people using apps such as Skype, then you will need to leave the "Allow access to the microphone on this device" to on as well as the "Allow apps to access your microphone". Under the "Choose which Microsoft Store apps can access your microphone", you will need to set the Skype app to "on". However, I do not use my microphone to communicate with anyone on my computer. Therefore, I set these settings to off. If you do use this feature, I highly encourage you to come back to this setting and ensure only the right apps have access to your microphone.

Voice Activation

Click on "Voice Activation". You will see "Allow apps to use voice activation", "Allow apps to use voice activation when this device is locked", and "Choose which apps can use voice activation". For each of these settings, we are going to switch them to off.

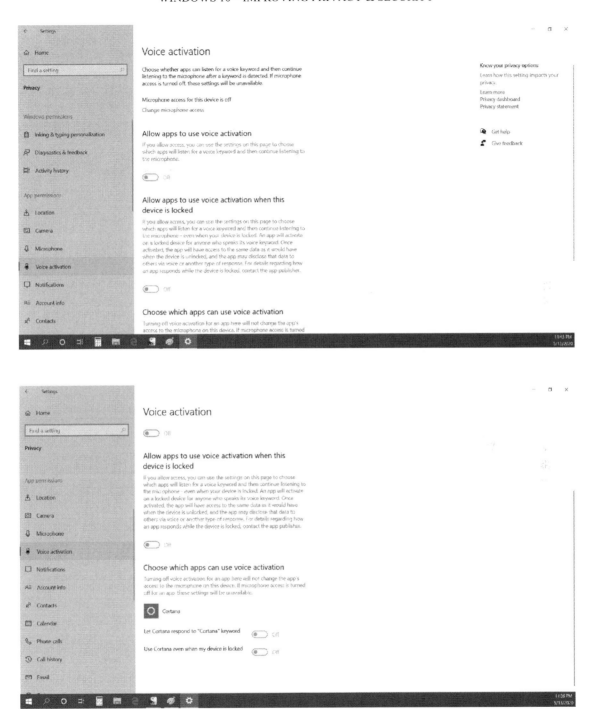

Notifications

Click on "Notifications". From here, you will see "Allow access to user notifications on this device" and "Allow apps to access your notifications". You will want to set both of these settings to off. We do not want our apps to have access to notifications from our system.

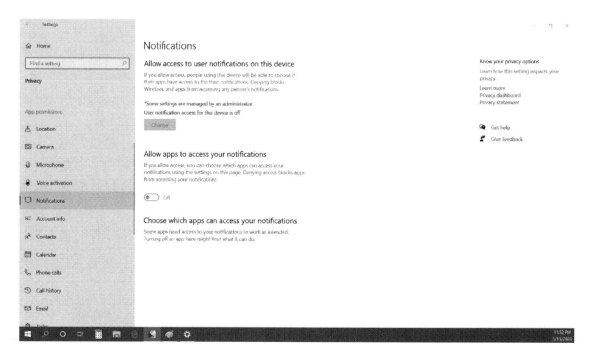

Account Info

Click on "Account Info". From here you will see "Allow access to account info on this device", "Allow apps to access your account info", and "Choose which apps can access your account info". You will want to set all of the settings to off. This prevents apps from gathering information about your account.

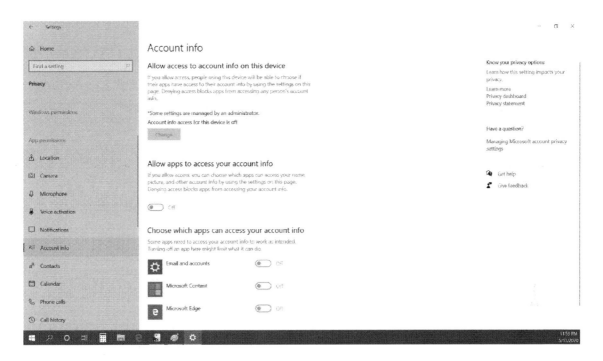

Contacts

Click on "Contacts". From here you will see "Allow access to contacts on this device", "Allow apps to access your contacts", and "Choose which apps can access your contacts". You will want to set all of the settings to off. This prevents apps from gathering information about your contacts.

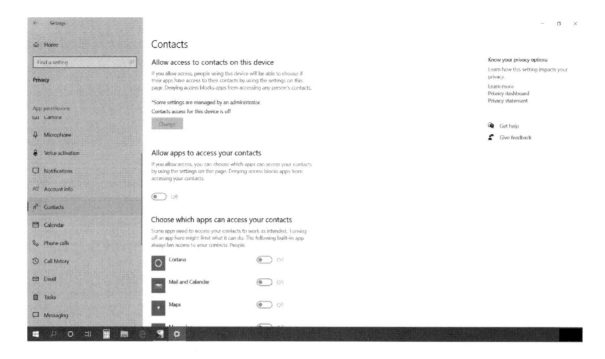

Calendar

Click on "Calendar". From here you will see "Allow access to calendars on this device", "Allow apps to access your calendar", and "Choose which apps can access your calendar". You will want to set all of the settings to off. This prevents apps from gathering information about your calendar.

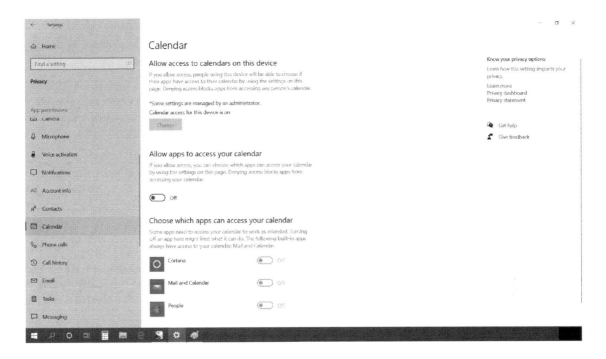

Phone Calls

Click on "Phone Calls". From here you will see "Allow phone calls on this device", "Allow apps to make phone calls", and "Choose which apps can make phone calls". You will want to set all of the settings to off. This prevents apps from gathering information about your phone calls.

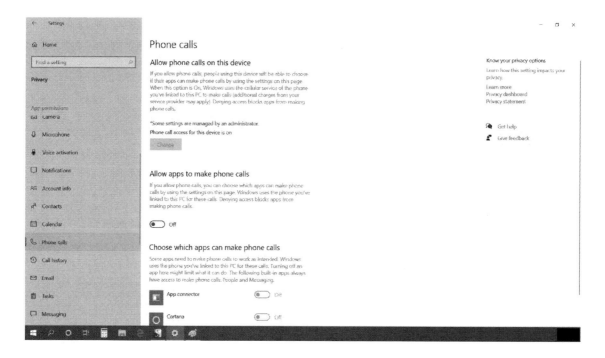

Call History

Click on "Call History". From here you will see "Allow access to call history on this device", "Allow apps to access your call history", and "Choose which apps can access your call history". You will want to set all of the settings to off. This prevents apps from gathering information about your call history.

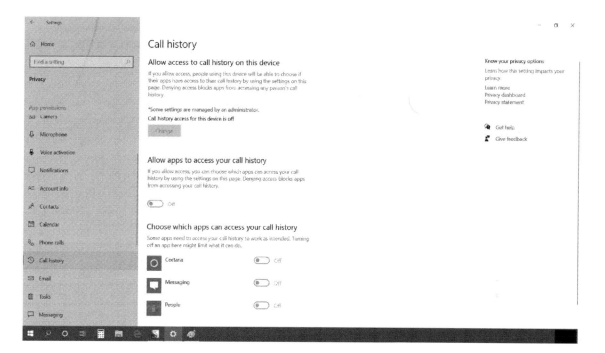

Email

Click on "Email". From here you will see "Allow access to email on this device", "Allow apps to access your email", and "Choose which apps can access your email". You will want to set all of the settings to off. This prevents apps from gathering information about your email.

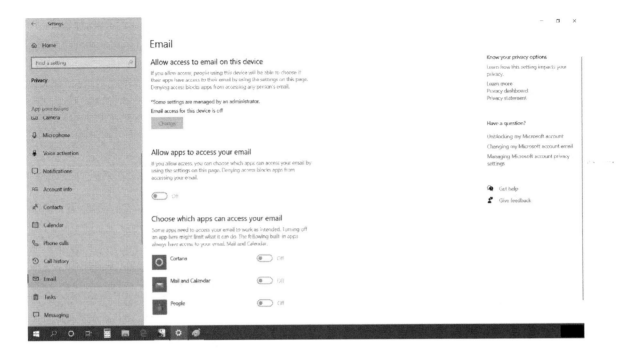

Tasks

Click on "Tasks". From here you will see "Allow access to tasks on this device", "Allow apps to access your tasks", and "Choose which apps can access your tasks". You will want to set all of the settings to off. This prevents apps from gathering information about your tasks.

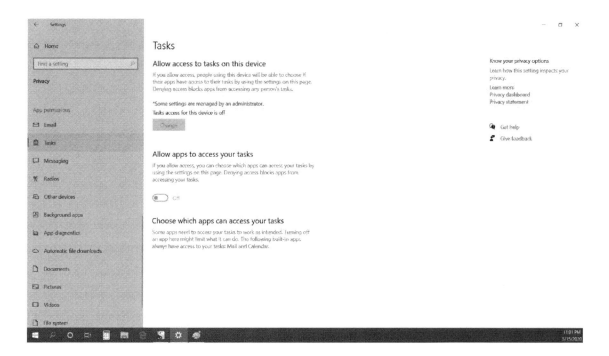

Messaging

Click on "Messaging". From here you will see "Allow access to messaging on this device", "Allow apps to read or send messages", and "Choose which apps can read or send messages". You will want to set all of the settings to off. This prevents apps from gathering information about your messages.

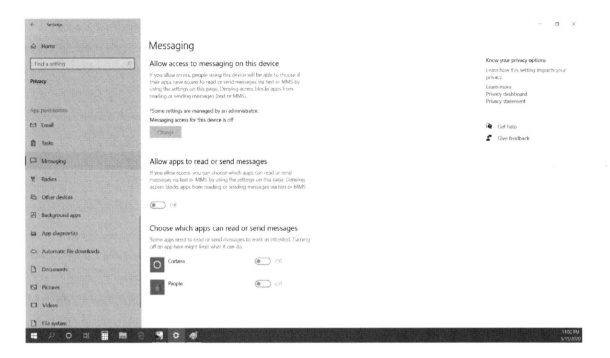

Radios

Click on "Radios". From here you will see "Allow access to control radios on this device", "Allow apps to control device radios", and "Choose which apps can control your device radios". You will want to set all of the settings to off. This prevents apps from gathering information about your radios.

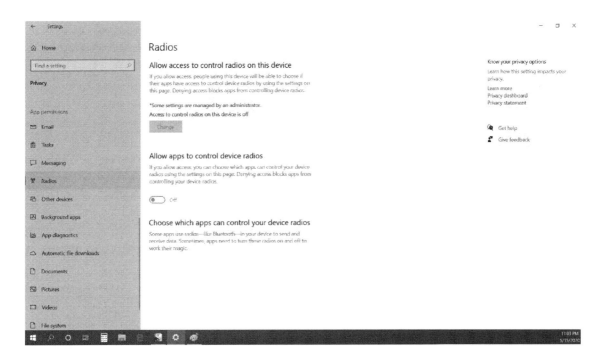

Other Devices

Click on "Other Devices". From here you will see "Communicate with unpaired devices" and "Use trusted devices". You will want to set "Communicate with unpaired devices" to off. Under "Use trusted devices", you will want to remove any devices you do not want as trusted. This prevents apps and third-party devices from tracking and using information from paired devices and unpaired devices.

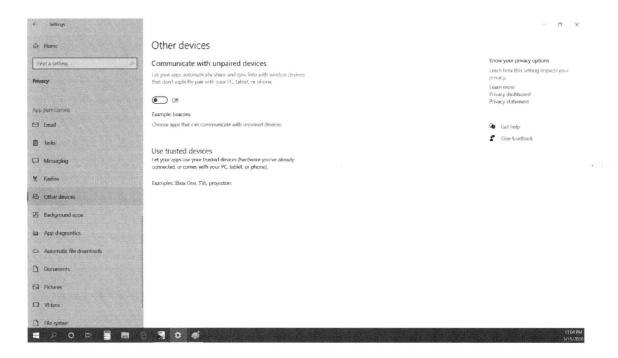

Background Apps

Click on "Background Apps". From here you will see "Background Apps" and "Choose which apps can run in the background". You will want to set all of the settings to off. This prevents apps from maliciously running in the background.

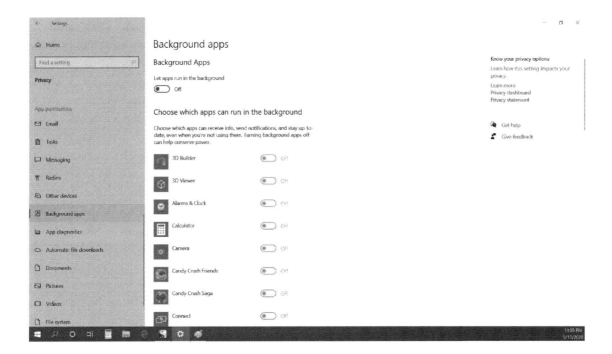

App Diagnostics

Click on "App Diagnostics". From here you will see "Allow access to app diagnostic info on this device", "Allow apps to access diagnostic info about your other apps", and "Choose which apps can access diagnostic info about other apps". You will want to set, all of the settings to off. This prevents apps from gathering information about your app diagnostic information.

Automatic File Downloads

Click on "Automatic File Downloads". From here you will see any apps which have access to file downloading capability. If apps appear in this window, this means they have privileges to download files. However, if you do not see any apps in this window, that means they do not have privileges to download files. Remove any unwanted apps here.

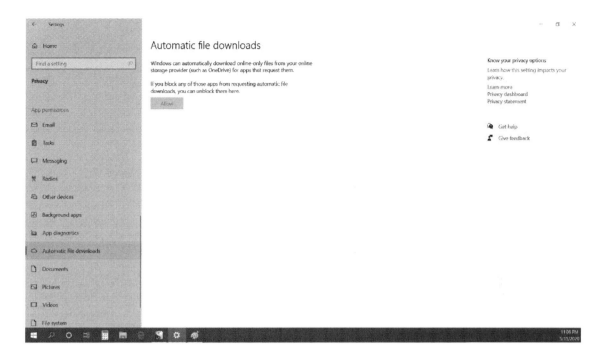

Documents

Click on "Documents". From here you will see "Allow access to document libraries on this device", "Allow apps to access your document library", and "Choose which apps can access your documents library". You will want to set all of the settings to off. This prevents apps from gathering information and access to your documents.

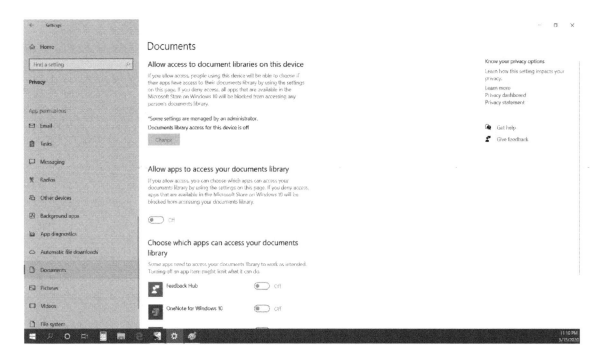

Pictures

Click on "Pictures". From here you will see "Allow access to picture libraries on this device", "Allow apps to access your pictures library", and "Choose which apps can access your pictures library". You will want to set all of the settings to off. This prevents apps from gathering information and access to your pictures.

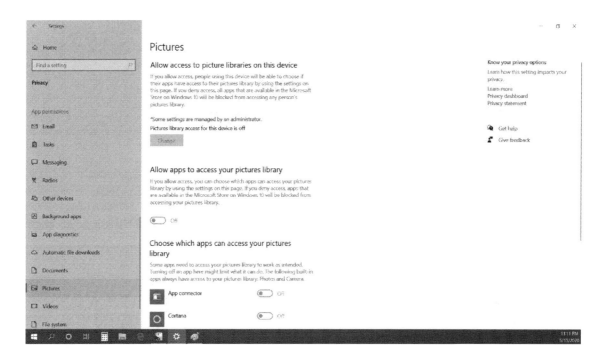

Videos

Click on "Videos". From here you will see "Allow access to video libraries on this device", "Allow apps to access your videos library", and "Choose which apps can access your videos library". You will want to set all of the settings to off. This prevents apps from gathering information and access to your videos.

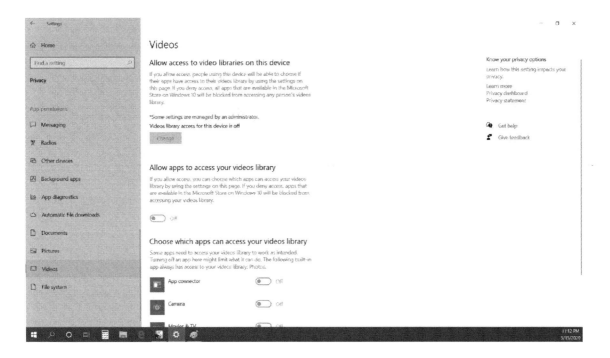

File System

Click on "File System". From here you will see "Allow access to the file system on this device", "Allow apps to access your file system", and "Choose which apps can access your file system". You will want to set all of the settings to off. This prevents apps from gathering information and access to your file system.

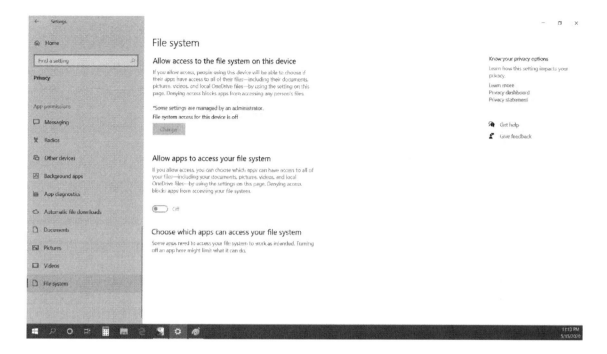

Privacy Overview

It is important to pay special attention to this section. Most information being monitored, gathered, and shared can be turned on or off here. Over time you will want to navigate back to this location and check to ensure these settings are still off. You may accidentally modify these settings over time so be careful and continue to review this location. After all, your computer has access to your locations, camera, microphone, calendar, call history, email, etc....

CHAPTER 06 – Network & Internet

In this chapter, we will be going through the "Network & Internet" settings. We will learn all of the features in this area where we can improve our system's security and privacy.

Network & Internet Overview

The Network & Internet window allows you to view, modify, and implement important settings such as:

- Status
- Wi-Fi
- Ethernet
- Dial-up
- VPN
- Airplane Mode
- Mobile Hotspot
- Data Usage
- Proxy

Note: We will only be going over the Wi-Fi, VPN, Mobile Hotspot, Data Usage, and Proxy. This is where you can make security and privacy enhancements.

Navigate to Network & Internet

Step 1: Click "Start".

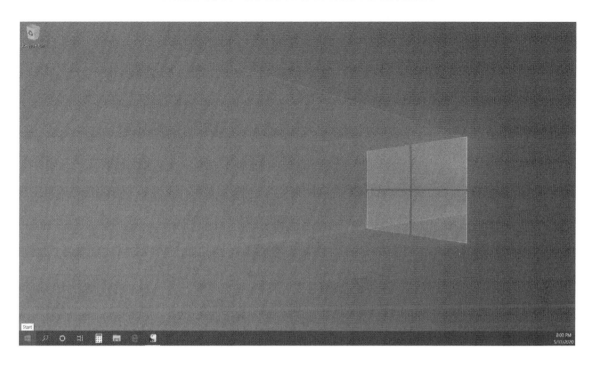

Step 2: Click "Settings".

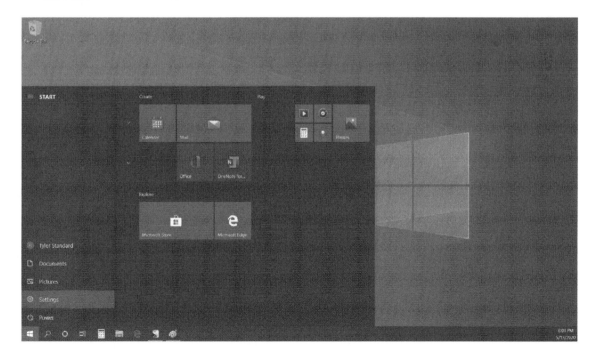

Step 3: Click "Network & Internet".

Network & Internet Settings

Wi-Fi: The Wi-Fi tab, shows you the current Wi-Fi connection status as well as available networks. You will see "Random Hardware Addresses". You will want to turn this on for "Use random hardware addresses". This will change the Wi-Fi hardware address for each new Wi-Fi connection you establish. This will prevent people from seeing your unique address across different Wi-Fi networks.

VPN: VPN stands for Virtual Private Network. VPN allows you to encrypt and protect the traffic going to and from your computer. This prevents Man-In-The-Middle attack scenarios. In this setting, you will want to set "Allow VPN over metered networks" and "Allow VPN while roaming" to On. To use this feature you will need VPN software/service. Go onto your favorite search engine and search for VPN software. This should return a good amount of services to select from. Once you have selected a free or paid for service go back to the VPN settings and click "Add a VPN connection". The VPN provider will provide you with the necessary information to establish the connection. Don't just pick any VPN provider. Make sure they are trustworthy and have good reviews. If you would like more information, please feel free to visit my website at www.TylerPayne.com for my latest VPN picks and reviews.

Mobile Hotspot: The Mobile Hotspot setting allows you to share your internet connection as well as allow remote control for turning on the hotspot. You will want to ensure the "Share my internet connection with other devices" and "Allow another device to turn on mobile hotspot" is set to off. You will want to come back to this setting throughout the year to ensure nothing has changed.

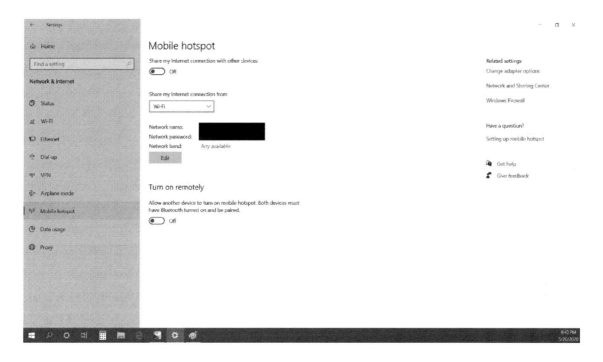

Data Usage: The Data Usage setting allows you to see how much data you are using over specific network connections. You can set limits, to the amount of data used over these connections. Under "Background Data", you will want to set the "Limit what Store apps and Windows features can do in the background" to "Always".

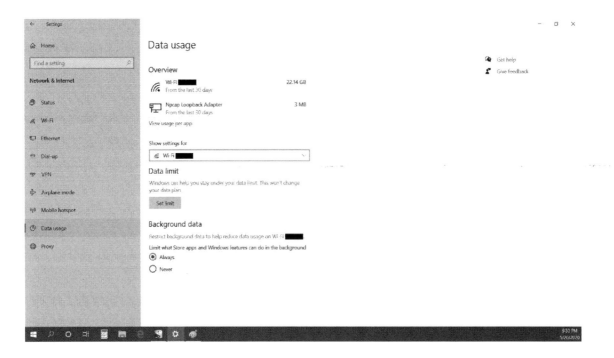

Proxy: A Proxy is referred to as a "Proxy Server". It acts as a gateway between your computer and the internet. When you visit a website, your request is sent to the proxy server. The proxy server acts on your computer's behalf. It provides a firewall and a filter that can block malicious content and Ads from getting to your computer. You will want to set "Automatically detect settings" and "Use setup script" to off.

If you would like to use a proxy, you will need to turn it on and provide a proxy server. Under "Manual proxy setup" you will want to set the "Use a proxy server" to On. However, just as the VPN setting, you will need to go on your favorite search engine and find a trusted proxy server. Once you have selected one, you will need to input the Address and Port. Be sure to save the settings when finished.

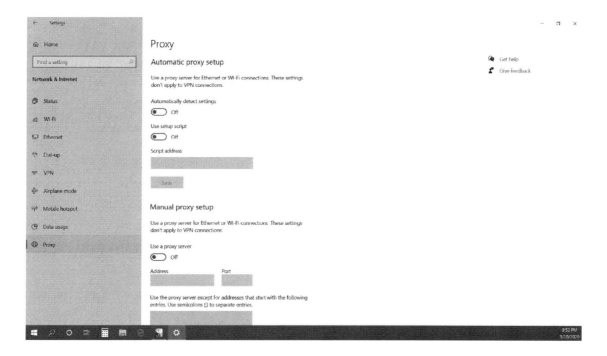

Network & Internet Review

As you can see, the "Network & Internet" section, has settings that can be used to increase security and privacy while connected to networks and browsing the web. The VPN is great for protecting the data you send and receive from the web. The Proxy acts as a firewall to protect your system from malicious content on the web. Don't forget, when you connect to Wi-Fi enabled networks, you want to be on a secure connection. An open connection leaves you open to attacks.

CHAPTER 07 – Microsoft Edge

In this chapter, we will discuss Microsoft's built-in web browser Microsoft Edge. Even though at the time of this publication, Microsoft's Web Browser "Internet Explorer 11" is also available; we are only going to discuss "Microsoft Edge". The reason, Internet Explorer 11 will fade away soon and will be replaced by Microsoft Edge. As of this publication, Microsoft Edge is still new. Therefore, websites need time to develop/modify their current compatibility settings to adjust for Microsoft Edge.

Microsoft Edge Overview

Microsoft Edge is Window's newest web browser. Microsoft Edge is supposed to replace Internet Explorer as a more secure user-friendly web browser. The Edge browser works hand in hand with Windows Defender and is considered the most secure browser for Windows 10. Currently, Internet Explorer 11 is still available for Windows 10. However, it is only a matter of time until websites stop supporting Internet Explorer 11. Microsoft Edge has certainly increased its security and here's how.

Sandbox: Microsoft Edge operates in a sandbox. For those unfamiliar with this term, a sandbox is an isolated process. Microsoft Edge operates in a virtual process, with limited permission, within the system. It has little to no rights with making permanent changes to the system.

Windows Defender Smart Screen: This is a great feature when protecting people while browsing the web. The Windows Defender Smart Screen can determine if a site is malicious, a file is malicious, and if an app is malicious. As mentioned earlier, Microsoft Edge works great with Windows Defender. When visiting a website, the Defender feature will analyze the website and compare it to a database of potentially dangerous web sites. If the site has been reported as dangerous, you will get a notification. This is the same process when downloading files and apps.

Navigate to Microsoft Edge

Step 1: Click on "Start".

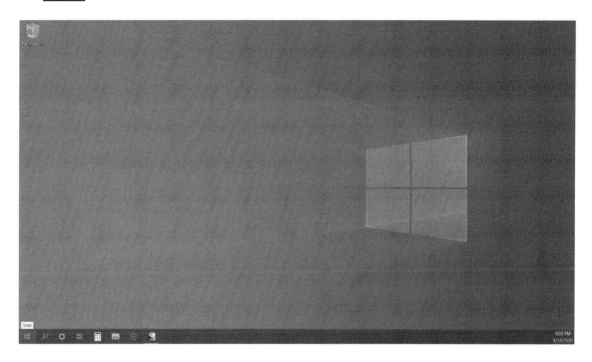

Step 2: Under programs, scroll down until you find the letter "M".

Step 3: Click on "Microsoft Edge".

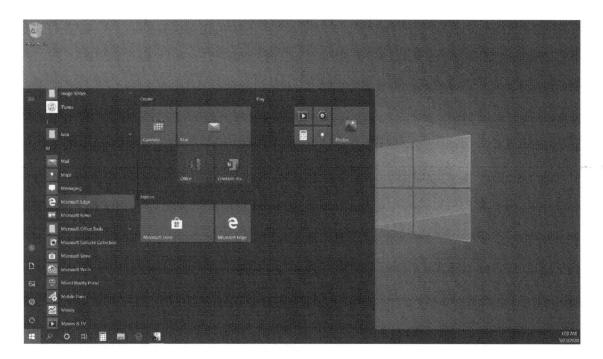

Microsoft Edge Settings

To use Microsoft Edge correctly. Please visit Chapter 8 "Isolated Browsing", to enable the "Application Guard".

Microsoft Edge Review

Microsoft Edge is Windows 10 newest and most secure browser. It no longer supports vulnerable code such as ActiveX. It has reduced the system's attack surface by operating in a sandbox. It protects people from malicious websites, files, and apps. If you haven't started using Microsoft Edge, my advice to you is to try it.

CHAPTER 08 – Windows Security

In this chapter, you will learn about the built-in "Windows Security" features and how to correctly set the features to enhance the computer's security posture.

Windows Security Overview

Windows Security comprises of seven protection areas used to secure the Windows OS and protect your personal information. The seven protection areas are:

- Virus & Threat Protection
- Account Protection
- Firewall & Network Protection
- App & Browser Control
- Device Security
- Device Performance & Health
- Family Options

However, we will only cover the first 4 protection areas.

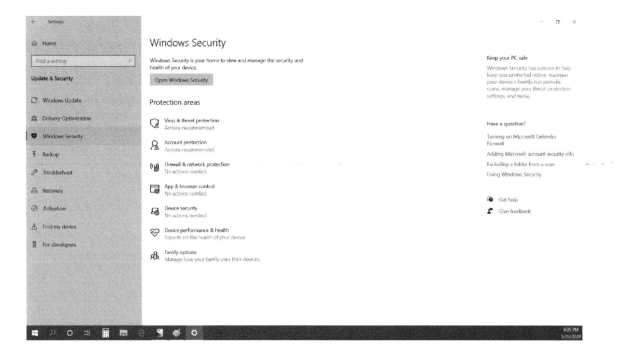

Navigate to Windows Security

Step 1: Click "Start".

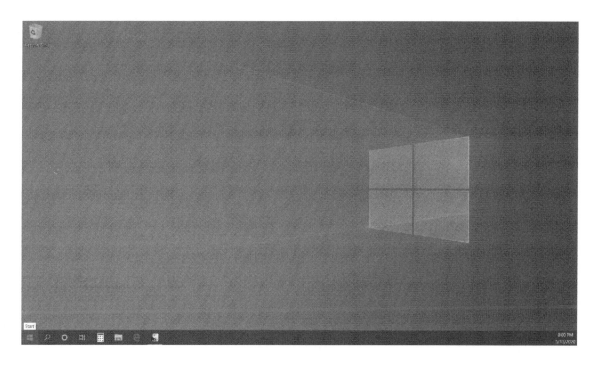

Step 2: Click "Settings".

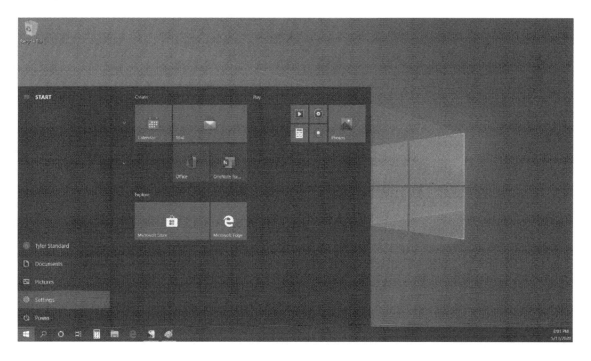

Step 3: Click "Update & Security".

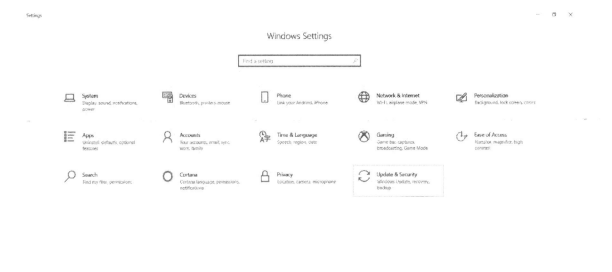

Step 4: Click "Windows Security".

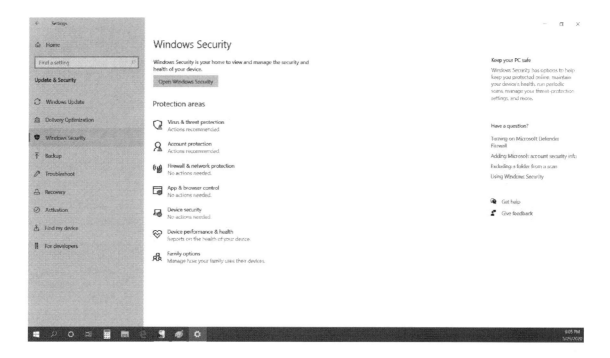

Virus and Threat Protection Overview

The Virus and Threat Protection protects against malware and ransomware. In this setting, you have the option to immediately perform a "Quick Scan". You can also adjust the scan options to perform a Full Scan, Custom Scan, and/or Offline Scan. You can look at the history of these scans and see what was found. You can check for updates and set up the OneDrive account to protect your system from ransomware.

Navigate to Virus and Threat Protection

Step 1: Click "Start".

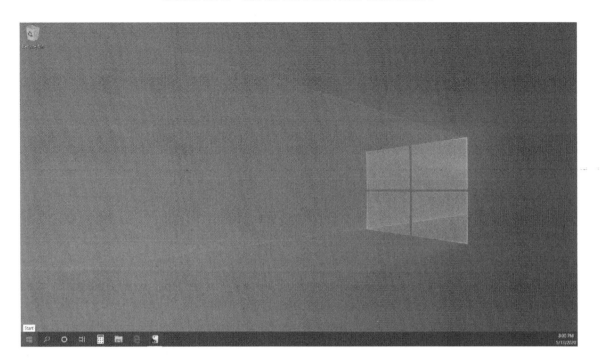

Step 2: Click "Settings".

Step 3: Click "Update & Security".

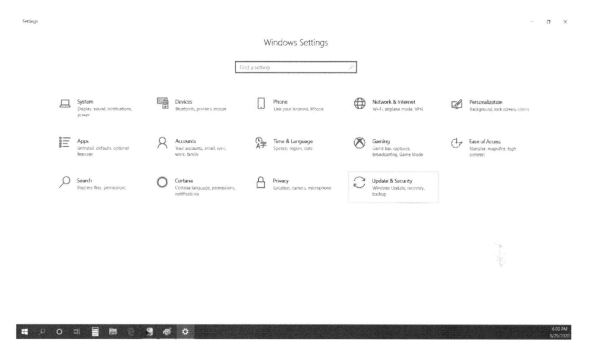

Step 4: Click "Windows Security".

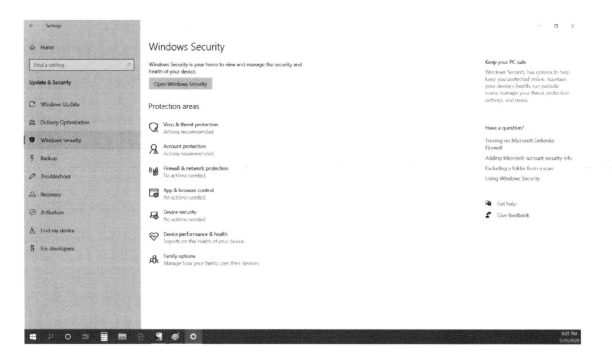

Step 5: Click "Virus & Threat Protection".

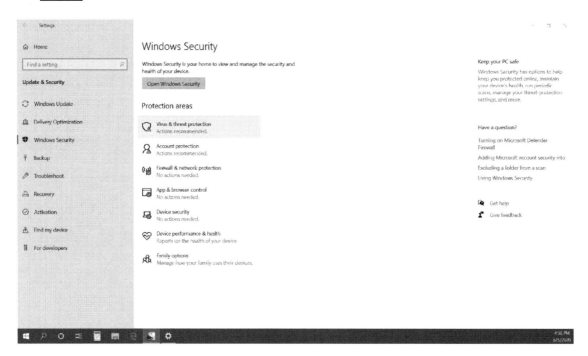

Virus and Threat Protection Settings

From this window, you will see "Current threats". From here you can do a quick scan to perform a threat scan of your system. In this window, you can see when the last scan was performed on the system and the number of files scanned. Further down you will see the "Virus & Threat Protection Settings", "Virus & Threat Protection Updates", and "Ransomware Protection".

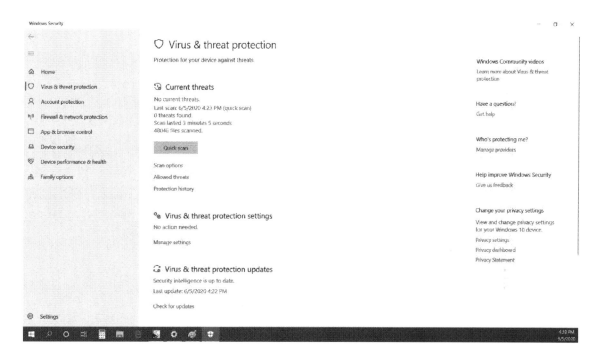

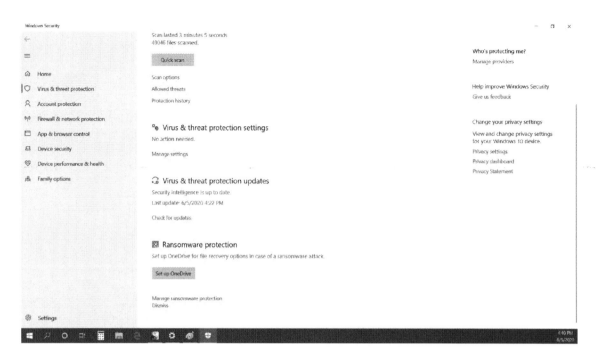

If you click on "Scan options", you will see the option to perform a Quick scan, Full scan, Custom scan, and Windows Defender Offline scan. A quick scan will do a pretty good job but it is recommended to perform a Full scan at least once a month.

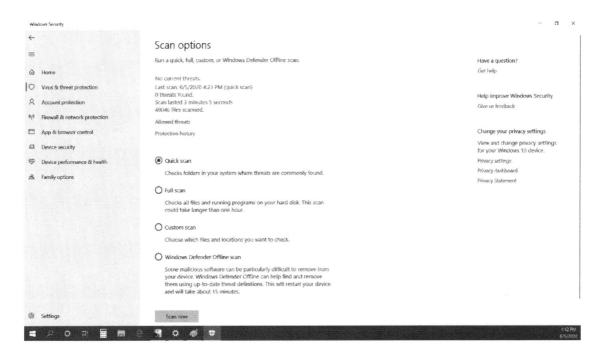

Under "Virus & Threat Protection Settings" you will want to click on "Manage Settings". From here you will want to ensure "Real-time Protection", "Cloud-delivered Protection", "Automatic Sample Submission", and "Tamper Protection" are all set to "On".

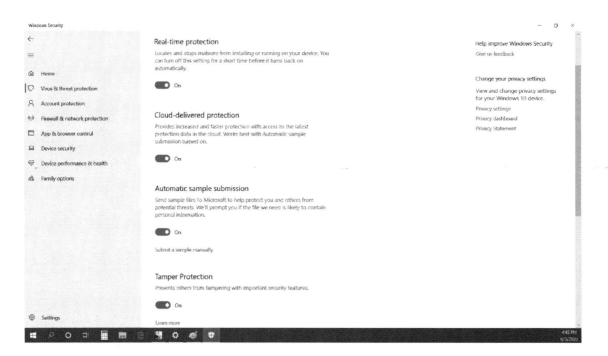

Under "Virus & threat protection updates", you can see the date for the last time the system updated its virus and threat protection database. I recommended you update within 30 days of the current calendar date.

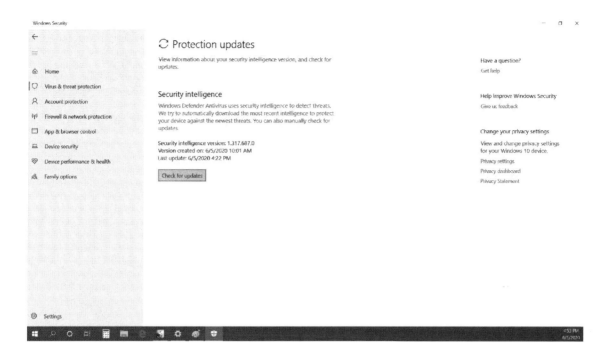

Under "Ransomware Protection", you should see "Set up OneDrive for file recovery options in case of a ransomware attack". However, if you see "No action needed", this means you already have Microsoft OneDrive setup and in use on the system. The OneDrive allows you to backup personal files on the computer. If the system becomes compromised due to a ransomware attack, you can easily restore your information from Microsoft OneDrive.

From here click on "Manage ransomware protection". You will see "Controlled folder access". Make sure this is set to on if you would like to protect your information from a Ransomware attack. Click on "Protected folders". From here you will see a list of all protected folders. You can click on each folder and click remove. However, some may be grayed out. You can also add a folder to protect by clicking on the plus sign next to "Add a protected folder".

Under "Ransomware data recovery", you will see the OneDrive email address used to back up your files. Take note of this email as you will need this to access your backups in case you fall victim to a Ransomware attack. You can also click on "View files" to see the current files that have already been backed-up to Microsoft OneDrive.

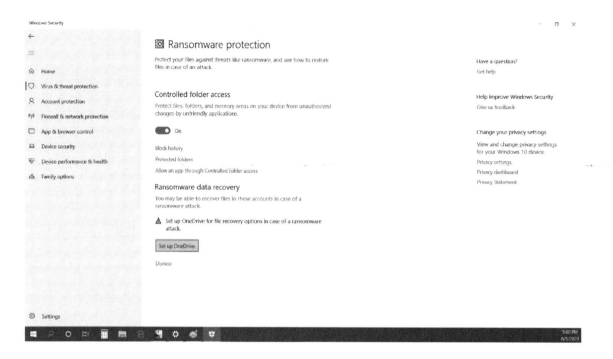

Note: I do not use Microsoft OneDrive as I backup my files to a local external hard drive. Microsoft OneDrive stores your data in the "Cloud" and I do not like my information being stored on the web.

Account Protection Overview

The Account Protection provides you with the option to use "Windows Hello". This feature can manage how you sign in to your device. The feature allows you to use "Windows Hello Face", "Windows Hello Fingerprint", "Windows Hello PIN", "Security Key", "Password", and "Picture Password". It also has "Dynamic Lock", which allows you to use Bluetooth on your computer and phone. If you step away from the computer with your phone, the computer will automatically lock.

Navigate to Account Protection

Step 1: Click "Start".

Step 2: Click "Settings".

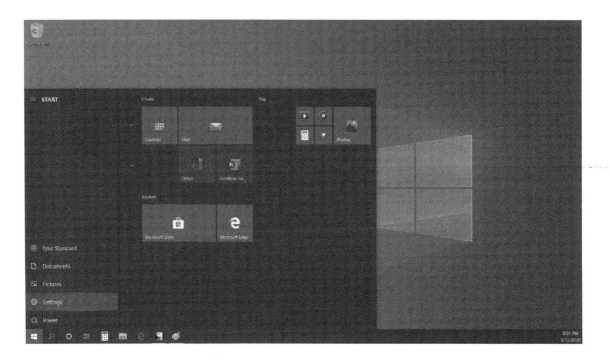

Step 3: Click "Update & Security".

Step 4: Click "Windows Security".

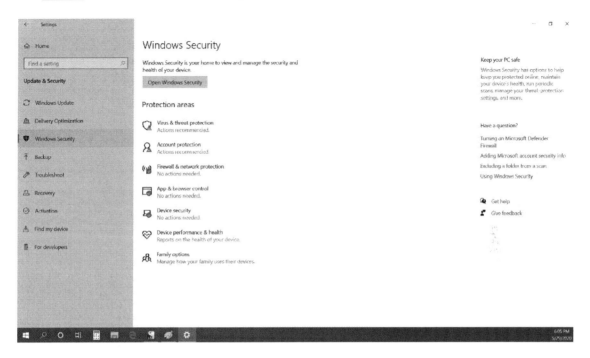

Step 5: Click "Account Protection".

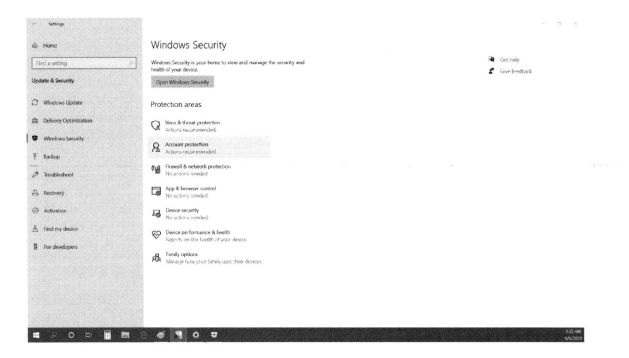

Account Protection Settings

Microsoft Account: The Microsoft Account provides additional capabilities to the computer such as the use of "Windows Hello". The security enhancements are stored in the cloud and provided to the computer when you sign-in using a Microsoft Account. I do not use this feature as I am not a fan of my information or security settings being stored in the cloud. However, if you are comfortable with this, by all means, try it. You may like it.

Windows Hello: You must be signed in to a Microsoft account to use this feature. This feature provides you the ability to sign-in, to your computer using facial recognition or PIN instead of a password. According to Microsoft, your face and PIN are only stored locally on the device and not in the cloud. My recommendation is if you are to use a Microsoft account with "Windows Hello", you should use the PIN feature. The PIN is stored within the TPM device as mentioned in the BitLocker Drive Encryption section of this book. It is more secure than the standard username and password. Facial recognition could be used. However, they sometimes provide false-positive access to individuals who have a similar style face.

Dynamic Lock: This setting provides you the option to pair your Bluetooth enabled phone with the computer. If you walk away from the computer with your Bluetooth enabled phone, the computer will automatically lock. This helps to secure the computer in case you accidentally walk away from the computer without locking it first.

To enable this, click on "Dynamic Lock Settings" and scroll down to "Dynamic Lock" and make sure the box is checked for "All Windows to automatically lock your device when you're away". You will be prompted to turn on Bluetooth and pair your device.

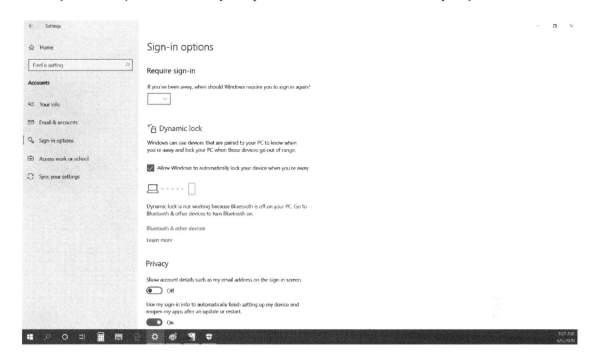

Firewall and Network Protection Overview

The Windows 10 Firewall & Network Protection provides you the capability to see what type of network the computer is connected to. According to Microsoft, the type is defined as either Domain Network, Private Network, or Public Network. You can think of Domain Network as the employer's workplace, Private Network as your home and Public Network as hotels, coffee shops, restaurants, etc.... This area allows you to set what is allowed in and out of the particular network.

Navigate to Firewall and Network Protection

Step 1: Click "Start".

Step 2: Click "Settings".

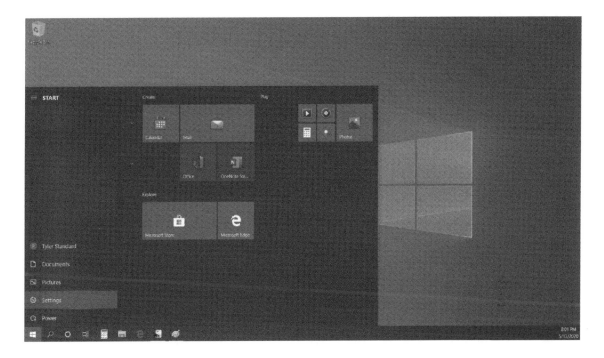

Step 3: Click "Update & Security".

Step 4: Click "Windows Security".

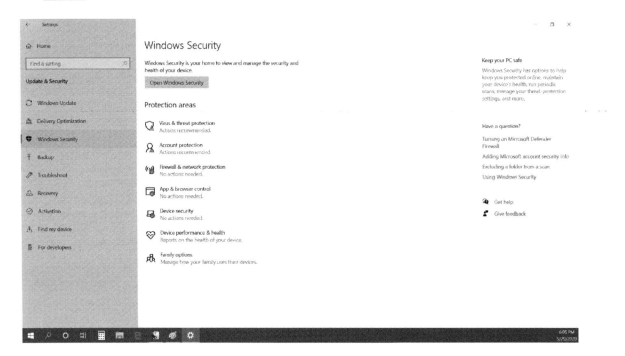

Step 5: Click "Firewall and Network Protection".

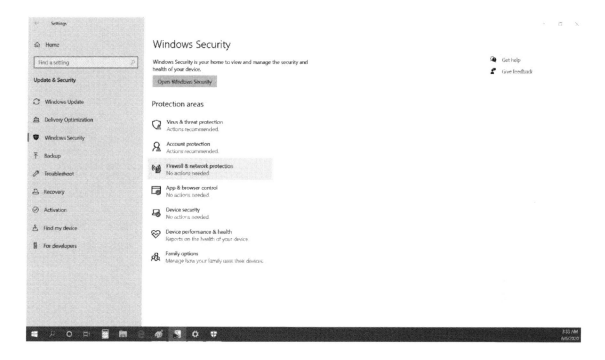

Firewall and Network Protection Settings

The settings for this area allow you to turn Windows firewall on or off for the Domain, Private, and Public network. It also allows you to specifically reject incoming connections for each particular network. You can also set which apps are allowed through the firewall, notifications, and set advanced settings for the firewall/network.

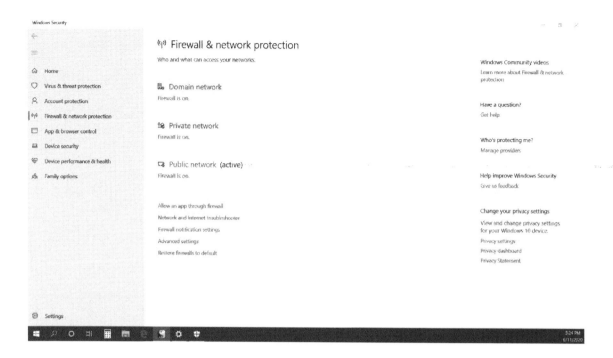

As you can see from the picture above. The network I am connected to is set as a "Public Network". However, this particular network is my home network. Whenever you make a new network connection, you are given the option to choose what type of network this connection will be. I choose "Public Network" for everything, as I do not like to share folders and files with anyone on the network. By setting it to a "Private Network", the firewall rules are less extensive because of Windows trust that you have a private connection. However, if someone were to hack into your network, you would become more vulnerable to the private network. This is because the "Private Network" is assumed to be trusted.

Domain Network: This network is mostly used by corporate companies. Some companies may allow **BYOD** (Bring Your Own Device). They allow you to bring your

personal computer and connect it to their network. Your computer will then receive system policies and settings from the Domain to meet special security settings/features.

Private Network: This network is mostly used for personal home networks. It makes sharing folders/files easier across the home network.

Public Network: This network is mostly used when connecting to public networks such as in the airport or your local coffee shop. However, you can set your home network to use this setting as it provides additional security.

Each network assignment provides different default security settings. However, each network can be tailored through additional settings.

Allow an App Through Firewall: The Firewall gives you the capability to allow or deny "apps and features" communication with your system. For instance, you can go into the firewall settings and remove "Cortana" from having access to the Internet.

Step 1: Click on "Allow an app through the firewall".

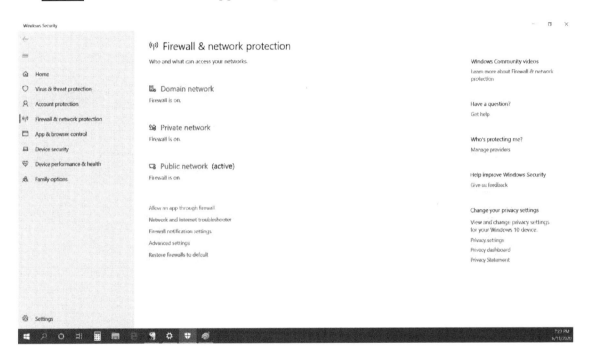

Step 2: Click on "Change Settings".

Step 3: Uncheck the "Private" and "Public" boxes for Cortana. Click "OK" when finished.

Note: You should go through all of the options listed and turn off what access to apps and features you do not want to communicate to and from your system. You may need to do a little research on the setting if you are unsure what you are about to uncheck as it may lead to system performance issues. You can always go back into the "Firewall & Network Protection" settings and click on "Restore Firewalls to Default" in the event you break something and can't remember how to undo the problem.

App & Browser Control Overview

The App & Browser Control section allows you to have Windows Defender monitor/warn/block apps by checking the apps against known malicious behavior on the web. You can also enable or disable Windows features such as "Defender Application Guard". The settings that can be modified here are:

- Check Apps and Files
- SmartScreen for Microsoft Edge
- SmartScreen for Microsoft Store Apps
- Isolated Browsing
- Exploit Protection

Navigate to App & Browser Control

Step 1: Click "Start".

Step 2: Click "Settings".

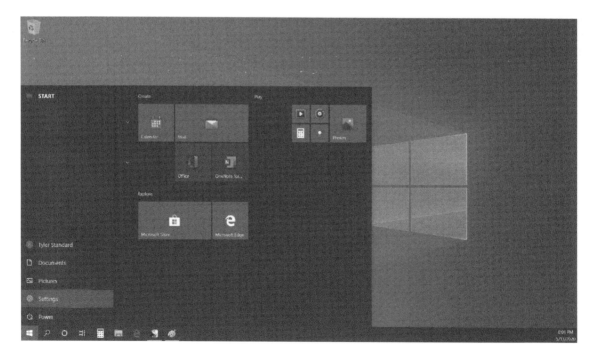

Step 3: Click "Update & Security".

Step 4: Click "Windows Security".

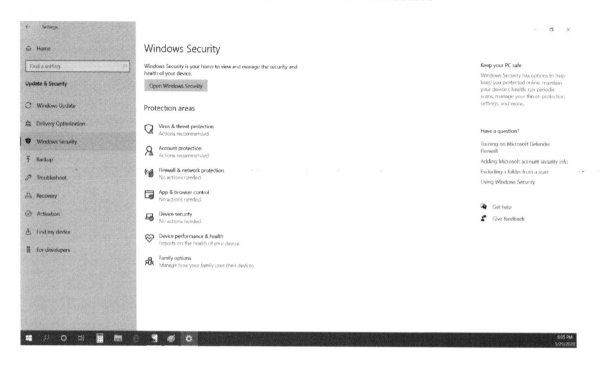

Step 5: Click "App & browser control".

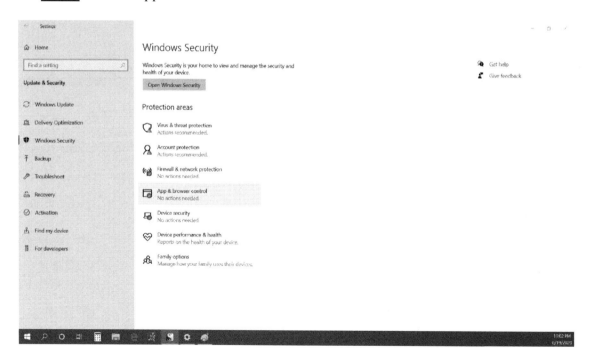

App & Browser Control Settings

Check apps and files: According to Windows 10, "Windows Defender SmartScreen helps protect your device by checking for unrecognized apps and files from the web.". You will want to set this setting to "Warn".

SmartScreen for Microsoft Edge: According to Windows 10, "Windows Defender SmartScreen Filter helps protect your device from malicious sites and downloads.". You will want to set this setting to "Warn".

SmartScreen for Microsoft Store apps: According to Windows 10, "Windows Defender SmartScreen protects your device by checking web content that Microsoft Store apps use.". You will want to set this setting to "Warn".

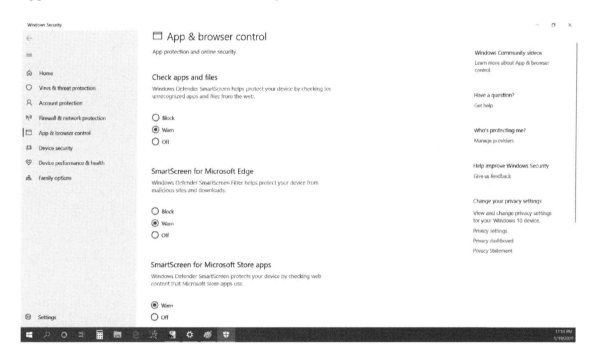

Isolated Browsing: According to Windows 10, "Windows Defender Application Guard opens Microsoft Edge in an isolated browsing environment to better protect your device and data from malware.".

Step 1: Click on "Install Windows Defender Application Guard".

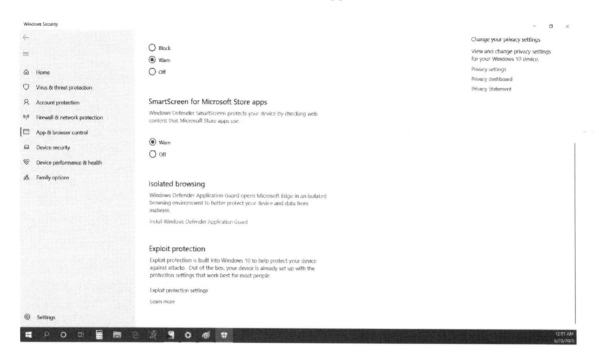

Step 2: Scroll down until you find "Windows Defender Application Guard". Click on the checkbox and click "Okay".

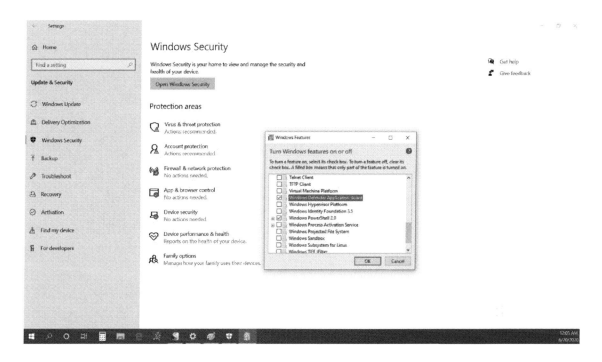

Step 3: When the installation is complete, you will be asked to restart the computer for the changes to take effect. Go ahead and click "Restart Now".

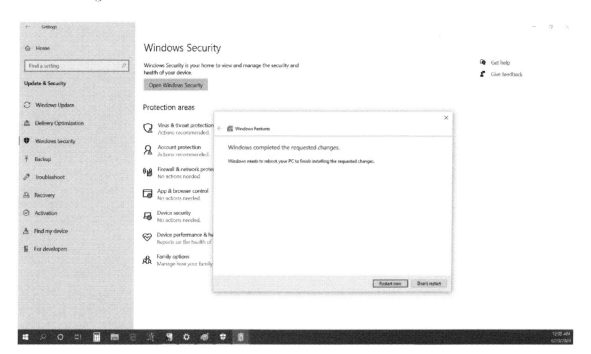

Step 4: After the computer is restarted, you will need to navigate back to the "App & Browser Control" settings. Under "Isolated Browsing", you should see "Change Application Guard Settings" and "Uninstall Windows Defender Application Guard".

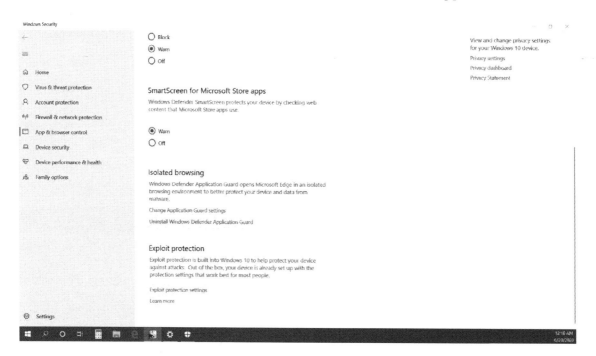

Step 5: Click on "Change Application Guard Settings". From here you will see Save Data, Copy and Paste, Print Files, Camera and Microphone, and Advanced Graphics. If you wish to Copy and Paste to and from Microsoft Edge, you will need to make sure this is set to On. My recommendation is to leave everything Off until you need to use one of these features and then turn it On. When you are done using the feature such as "Print Files" you will want to turn it back off.

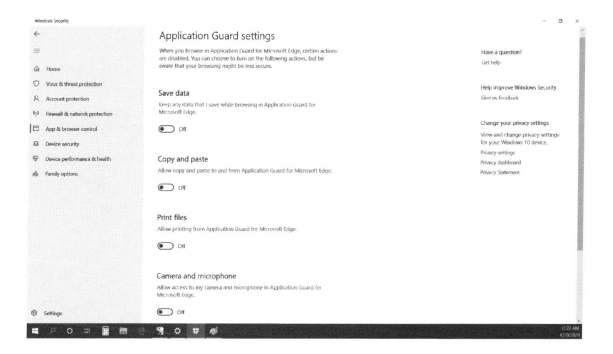

Exploit Protection: According to Windows 10, "Exploit protection is built into Windows 10 to help protect your device against attacks. Out of the box, your device is already set up with the protection settings that work best for most people.".

- Click on Exploit protection settings and ensure Control Flow Guard, Data Execution Prevention, Force Randomization for Images, Randomize Memory Allocations, High-entropy ASLR, Validate Exception Chains, and Validate Heap Integrity are all set to "Use Default (On).

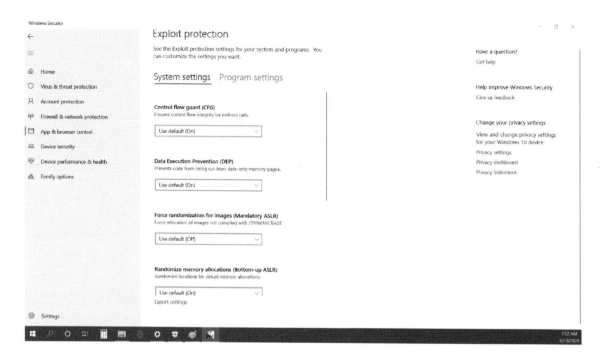

Windows Security Review

In this chapter, we covered how you can utilize the Virus & Threat Protection, Account Protection, Firewall & Network Protection, and the App & Browser Control protection features. These features provide us the capability to protect our system from malware, ransomware, and programs such as Remote Access Tools (RAT). We can also use the Firewall to prevent incoming and outgoing connections over a network. This section provides many security features for protecting our system and personal information.

CHAPTER 09 – Backup & Recovery

In this chapter, you will learn the most important step when dealing with security and data. Having a good Backup and Recovery process is key when dealing with situations such as hard drive corruption or ransomware. The ability to quickly and effectively get your computer up and running from a hardware disaster or theft is key when dealing with these types of situations.

Backup & Recovery Overview

Windows 10 provides an easy to use backup and recovery feature. With Windows 10, you can select folders you wish to back up and folders you wish to exclude from backups. You can set how often you wish the folders to be backed up and how long you wish to keep your backups. Windows 10 also provides an easy restore feature for restoring missing or corrupted folders.

Navigate to Backup

Step 1: Click "Start"

Step 2: Click "Settings"

Step 3: Click "Update & Security"

Step 3: Click "Backup"

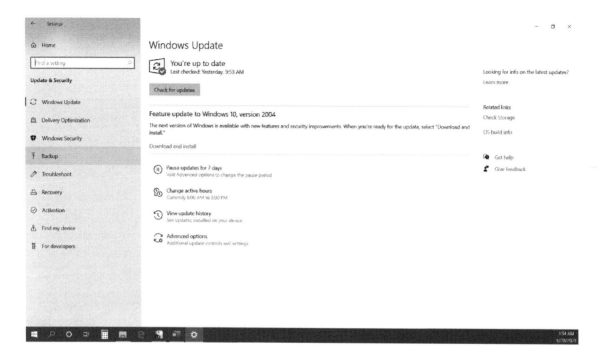

Backup Settings

Here we will backup files on the computer to a secondary hard drive.

Step 1: Under "Back up Using File History", click "Add a Drive". A window will open asking you to select the drive you wish to back the files up to. You must have an external USB drive plugged into the system or a second internal hard drive.

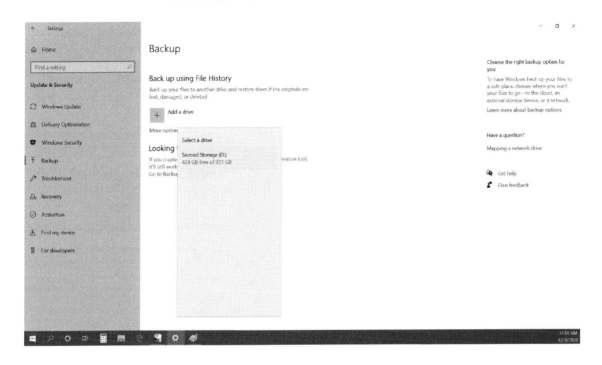

Step 2: Under "Back Up Using File History", click on "More Options".

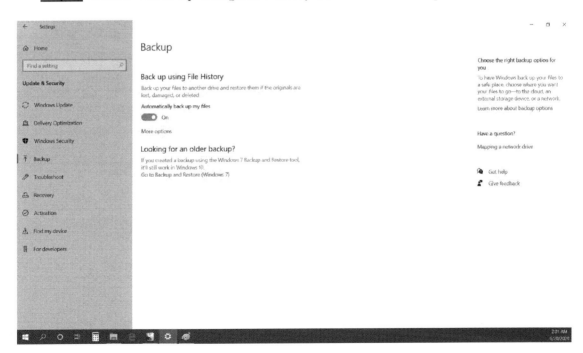

Step 3: The folders which will be backed up are listed under "Back-Up These Folders". If you see a folder you do not wish to backup, click on the folder and click "Remove".

Step 4: If you wish to back up a folder not listed under the "Back Up These Folders", you will want to click on "Add a Folder". The "Select Folder" window will open. You will want to click on the desired folder and click "Choose This Folder".

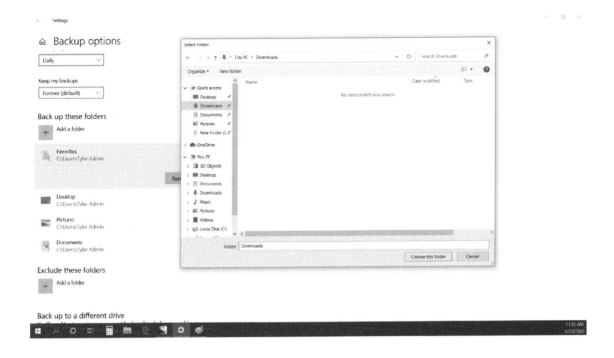

Step 5: Under "Overview", you can set when and how long to keep files backed up. Under "Back Up Files", I set mine to "Daily" and under "Keep My Backups", I leave it at the default setting "Forever". When ready, you will need to click "Back Up Now".

Step 6: Now if you navigate to the drive you selected, you will see a folder called "FileHistory". This is the location of the folders you have just backed up. Mine was located on the D: drive > FileHistory > Tyler Admin.

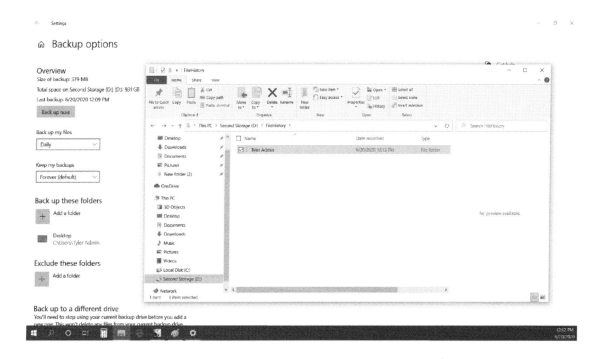

Restore Files from a Current Backup Setting

Here we will restore a file from a previous backup.

Step 1: Navigate to "Backup" and click "More Options", as described in Step 2 of "Backup Settings". At the bottom click on "Restore Files from a Current Backup".

Step 2: Click on the folder you wish to restore and then click on the green counter-clockwise button at the bottom. For this restore, I have chosen to restore the Music folder.

Step 3: You may see a window open asking you, "Replace the Files in The Destination", "Skip These Files", and "Let Me Decide for Each File". Be careful not to overwrite anything that may be newer than the previous backup. You can click on "Let Me Decide for Each File", to ensure you know what file is being replaced. You can now navigate to the folder you selected and see the files are now restored.

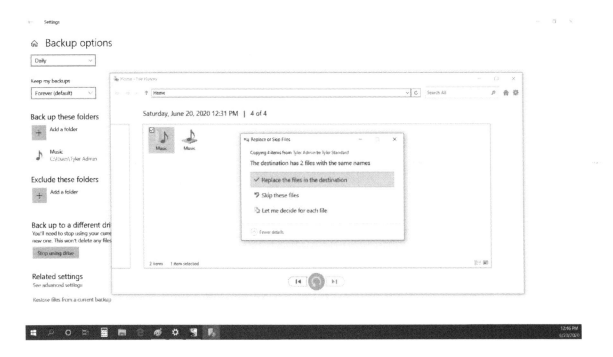

Backup & Recovery Review

In this chapter, we went through the process of creating a backup and restoring files from the backup. You were able to see how easy it is to create a backup, by including and excluding particular folders. You also learned how to restore a folder, in the event you accidentally delete a folder or file. Having a good backup and restore process is a key attribute, for a disaster recovery plan. You never know when your system will fail, a file may become corrupted, or fall victim to ransomware.

Made in the USA
Middletown, DE
28 March 2021